BEST NEBRASKA TEEN WRITING

2020

BEST NEBRASKA TEEN WRITING

2020

Hastings College Press | Hastings, Nebraska

ISBN-13: 978-1-942885-74-0

Manufactured in the United States of America.

Contents

Novel Writing

Personal Essay & Memoir

Poetry

Flash Fiction

Short Story

Humor

Introduction

In 2019, Hastings College launched the Nebraska Scholastic Writing Awards, becoming the first Nebraska school in many years to be an Affiliate Partner of the Alliance for Young Artists & Writers. We invited students age 13 and above from all 93 counties within the state of Nebraska to submit their writing in one of eleven categories, such as Critical Essay, Poetry, and Short Story. Graduating seniors also had the option of submitting a Writing Portfolio, a collection of works that demonstrate the writer's technical versatility. We received over 110 submissions in this inaugural year of the program, all of which were read by a jury of Hastings College faculty, staff, and students. The original work featured in this publication showcases the creativity of our 18 award recipients, whom we celebrated at an Awards Ceremony on campus that featured the Nebraska State Poet, Matt Mason, as keynote speaker.

The Scholastic Art & Writing Awards program, established in 1923 by Maurice R. Robinson, the founder of Scholastic Inc., identifies teenagers with exceptional artistic and literary talent and brings their remarkable work to a national audience. All works are blindly adjudicated based on originality, technical skill, and the emergence of personal vision or voice, first on a regional level by more than 100 local affiliates of the Alliance, and then nationally by an impressive panel of industry experts. Students at the regional level are awarded an Honorable Mention, Silver Key, or Gold Key distinction. Gold Key work then advances to national adjudication to receive Gold Medals or Silver Medals. Each region also nominates works for American Voices & Visions Medals, the highest regional honor.

Annually, the Alliance partners with individuals, foundations, and corporations to offer scholarship opportunities for students in certain categories or addressing particular themes. National Medalists' works are published in national publications and on the Alliance's website, artandwriting.org. Select writing is published in *The Best Teen Writing* annual anthology. The Alliance strives to teach young students to develop a strong creative capacity along with celebrating the role of art and literature in society.

Dr. Eleanor Reeds
Hastings College
Hastings, NE

THE "ALPACA"LYPSE

OLIVIA ACHTEMEIER

Grade 9. Beatrice High School, Beatrice, NE. Jodi Fakler, Educator. *Gold Key.*

"Thump. Thump. Thump." The pencils on my desk fall to the floor. The lights turn off, then immediately back on again. I know it is here. The monster I had seen all over the news.

"Get going ..." I mumble to myself. I had to retreat to a safer area. Hoping for the best, I grab my bag and head out the door of my apartment.

Somewhere on the outskirts of town ...

"William, you started this," an employer at S.S. Laboratories chastised, "and now you're gonna get us out of it." A little over a week ago, William's branch of research (genetic engineering) was assigned the task of solving a large-scale problem. Well, okay, it more or less became a large-scale problem. They were asked to create clarity in today's society between the llama and the alpaca. To the scientists that work there, it was originally an honor to hear they would be dealing with this epic struggle.

From day one, they had a meeting in the department over reasonable solutions. "We just need to genetically enhance it in some way," a coworker of William's said.

"What about giving alpacas a bald spot?" someone suggested.

"We could make llamas' eyes blue and alpacas' eyes brown," another chimed in.

"What if we had alpacas be left-handed while llamas could be righties?" another said. This continued for a few minutes.

"We could give llamas extra teeth," Amanda suggested. You must know that William has never been very fond of her; she always seems to come up with genius ideas, which make him look bad. So he knew he had to beat her at brainstorming.

"What if," William spoke hesitantly, "llamas become smaller than alpacas?" Everyone's chatter stopped to look at him.

"Sounds good to me," Amanda said, although he knew what she really meant was, "*outstanding job, William. That is an amazing idea.*" The rest of the group agreed to give it a try.

So the next couple of days the group got to work. By the third day of strenuous research, they had a prototype. William watched as some of his fellow researchers entered a room, carrying a capsule of blue liquid. They gently poured it upon the readily waiting plush toy animal and, sure enough, it shrunk. William excitedly started to enter the testing area, but he saw it shockingly jump back to its original size. It, alas, was only temporary.

Many days went on like this until the scientists had another meeting. "We need to come up with a better solution," the discussion began. It continued much like the preceding group consultation. That is, until William had another idea.

"Rather than making llamas smaller, what if we make alpacas larger?" he astutely reasoned. Much like before, everyone agreed. The meeting was once again followed by a few days of testing until they had created a green liquid. This worked better than they had originally thought and, honestly, too well. William had been watching from behind a wall of glass. By now they were able to get a live alpaca to try the serum on. So he watched as it was injected into the animal.

"Um, William?" one of the men in a hazmat suit said through a small microphone.

"Yes?" he responded.

"I don't think this formula works either." His words gave William disappointment, but before he could feel much sorrow, the alpaca shot up a foot or two.

"It works!" he gleefully remarked. "It actually works!" William sees the man within the glass cautiously walk backwards. "Is something wron ..." Before he got a chance to finish the statement, the alpaca sprouted a couple more inches. Then it grew a few more feet. Eventually its head softly brushed the ceiling. William knew what he had to do. His hand reached over and yanked the trigger to evacuate the building. As people rushed out, he heard a large crash, and as he glanced back, the animal had reached preposterous proportions.

Back in an apartment building downtown ...

"Code Thirteen," the speakers directly above me muffle. "I repeat ... Code Thirteen." I continue walking as apartment doors fling open and numerous people of all ages flood the hallway. Although the chance of survival seems low to most, I know the odds are stacked even further against me due to my severe llama allergy. I made my way for the congested staircase as the speaker came on again: "The Beast is on 7th Street and heading towards 5th Street." It was only a matter of minutes until it reached 2nd Street, my street. I was shoved to the door, and I pushed it open.

The people around me scattered, but I pause to think. *Where did I park my car?* Before I have a chance to answer my question, the streets grow dark, and the air is filled with the smell of a petting zoo.

I look to my left and there the monster stands, two blocks away. The streets are swarmed by people. I followed in the direction they ran away from this monstrosity. Unfortunately it's no use. The Beast towers more than seven stories high. My two legs are no match compared to four. I fumble through my bag, and, sure enough, I find what I am looking for. I had slowed down and suddenly felt something soft touch me, then consume me. It was the Beast's legs. I jump to face it and spray all the llama repellent I have left in the container. To my disappointment, it remains unperturbed.

I panic. I was never taught what to do in a situation like this. I grip the curly fur of the animal, ready for it to move. I hold my breath, but nothing happens. I slowly look up, afraid of what I might see. Its head, a massive thing of fluff, was cocked downward, and its eyelids were closed. Everyone grew silent.

"Incredible!" a woman exclaimed in disbelief. "It finally fell asleep!" Her voice was heard within the mass of frozen humans. In shock, I stumble away from this wild animal. *Why hadn't I had an allergic reaction?*

A gigantic snort echoes through the buildings, and I see the llama's eyes shoot open. It begins to stomp, shaking the cement below my feet. Screams are heard all around. *My car is in the alley!* I recall. *That's not too far off.* I head into a narrow street, grab my keys, get in my car, a small truck, and drive fast. As I am exiting the alleyway, my vehicle comes to a sudden stop. Cars are all over the street, going nowhere.

"Why must the traffic be so bad at a time like this?" I say to myself. The creature is only a block away. Getting in my truck proved to kill time, not buy it. Throwing my purse in the back seat and hopping out of the car, I dodge various automobiles, bikes, and human beings. Then, much like before, everything stops. The llama leans its head forward into the street I am on. You can hear its steady breaths. In and out, in and out. A strange moaning sound emits from the Beast. Was this some sort of war cry?

From then on things could only get worse. A clear, slime-like liquid spouts from its mouth. Within only minutes, this repulsive smelling goop is everywhere. It splatters upon me. Although I can't identify this substance, I know it has to be a biohazard not only to me but also to everyone else. So I do all I can: wipe it off with my hands and keep sprinting. It progresses down the street, and I am aware of the fact that I cannot keep up the pace I am running at for long. I begin to slow down, and I hear a noise.

"Swishhh. Swishhh." I glance behind me to find that the llama is shaking from side to side. "Swishh. Swishh." It looked like a dog that had just taken a bath. Looking even further up, I see a small helicopter with buckets full of some sort of blue liquid. The fluid was being poured onto the alpaca's fur coat. And, just like something out of a story book, the animal shrunk. I am baffled and can hardly believe it. It is still humongous, but nonetheless smaller than before. I feel frozen in place.

Another helicopter swoops overhead, and, like the first, it has numerous buckets of the same liquid. The people, who from a distance were just small specs, empty the buckets' contents on the now sleek fur of the llama. The same astonishing thing occurred. It is now half the size it was earlier! Two more helicopters arrive. They follow the example of the others. So the creature was down to about twelve feet tall, but, before more liquid could be poured, it darts away, swifter than before. It speeds past me and turns left down a different street. The tables have turned, and I start to chase the animal, eager to see how this would play out. It gracefully gallops, but something happens. It appears to grow an inch or two. *The liquid must be temporary.*

A white van pulls up in an attempt to corner the llama, and it makes that same peculiar moaning noise and runs in the other direction, but more vans drift into the street. The creature is trapped but still growing. A woman in a lab coat steps out of the first van with an important looking briefcase. She bends down to her knees and pops the case open. From the distance, I can see what seems to be a syringe with a bright orange substance in it. A huge needle is at the end of it, and just the look of it gives me chills. The woman walks closer to the animal with the syringe in hand and makes shushing sounds. Her hand gently touches the soft, curly fur of the llama and jabs the needle into its shoulder. It starts to shrink back to an average size. I simply watch as a zookeeper comes into the scene with a rope. He gently ties it to the now normal zoo animal and walks with it into a van.

"Hey! Where did that llama come from?" I shout to the woman.

"It's an alpaca," she shouts back. Then she gets in the van without truly answering my question. As the vehicle drives off, I can't help but contemplate all that had just occurred. *So that's why my allergies didn't flare up.* I trudge back to my truck, finding that traffic has sped up again. When I arrive at my apartment, I turn on the television and watch the news report. The headline says that a disproportionate porcupine is on the loose.

A man from S.S. Laboratories is in the background yelling, "It's a hedgehog!"

The Greater Good

ELIZABETH GRANTHAM

Grade 12. Westside High School, Omaha, NE. Liz Hough, Educator. *Honorable Mention.*

Bergin always knew his brother was blessed. Throughout his entire life, Prince Palo had proven himself to have all the makings of a future leader: strength, courage, intelligence, mercy, and above all a deep and thorough understanding of the kingdom's motto, *for the greater good.* But it was only now, seconds away from having to fight quite possibly the bloodiest battle he ever had been in, that Bergin truly realized this.

"Soldiers of Cordona!" Palo boomed, his voice cracking from the sheer effort of making himself heard among the hundreds of people who stood before him. "Today is not a day we should fear! It is one we should celebrate! For today we take back the land the barbarians stole from us! We free the people—*our* people—who were captured and made slaves! We drive them out—*out!*—of our land, out of our country, and out of our homes once and for all!"

The army erupted into cheering, but Palo wasn't quite finished yet. He wheeled his horse around in a circle and held up his hands for silence.

"There are some," the prince continued somberly after the men had gone quiet, "who think there is no point to this war. They think it is a waste of blood and life, sweat and tears, a useless attempt to gain back a meaningless chunk of land. Well, I say they are wrong! Every life is precious! Every life is valuable and worthwhile! Only cowards would sit back in their safe, cozy homes and merely *watch* as their fellow countrymen suffer at the hands of ruthless barbarians! We are not cowards! We are brave and strong, and we will do whatever it takes to free our people and to fight, not just for ourselves, not just for our kingdom, but for the greater good! Are you with me!?"

The soldiers roared their approval, banging their weapons as hard as they could, making so much noise and commotion it seemed as if the entire earth echoed from their shouts. Bergin didn't care. He clashed his sword against his shield just like the rest of them, eager and ready to fight along his older brother's side.

"Then attack!"

The men didn't need to be told twice. A thousand bodies swarmed together, screaming as they charged down the hill into the city below, fully prepared to either take back what was theirs or else die in the process.

Bergin grinned. A rush of excitement shot down his spine and he urged his horse on even more. With every second he rode, the city became closer and closer until quite suddenly, it was right in front of him. Palo continued to lead the charge, crashing down the weak, wooden gate with his horse and galloping into the streets with a bare sword, but Bergin was right behind him. After all, he might not have been the heir, but he was still a prince of Cordona and he, too, had a responsibility to lead the soldiers into battle.

"For Cordona!" Bergin thundered, thrusting his blade into a nearby barbarian. "For the greater good!"

Some of the soldiers around him took up the cry, but most were too busy fighting to pay attention. The barbarians, despite being attacked so unexpectedly, had amazingly managed to round up their weapons in an incredible amount of time and were now fighting back with just as much viciousness as the Cordonians.

Bergin furrowed his brow. That was odd. Most people who were caught unprepared in a battle often *scrambled* to defend themselves. Yet the barbarians—

A sudden force slammed into his back, interrupting his thoughts, and Bergin let out a sharp cry of pain. Normally he was an excellent rider, but in this case he completely lost his balance and slipped and fell off his horse.

"Not so tough without your pretty, little stallion, are yah, boy?" asked a new voice, harsh and grating to the ears.

Bergin jumped to his feet, just in time to avoid the axe of a tall, heavyset barbarian who was wildly swinging it at him.

"You killed mah friend back der, didha know dat!?" the man asked, brandishing his weapon once again, only this time much harder.

Bergin sidestepped easily and grabbed the barbarian by the forearm. "So? You killed my people *and* you knocked me off my horse."

He gave the forearm a sharp twist and its owner bellowed in pain. Bergin lost no time. Quickly, while he was still distracted, the prince drew his sword and plunged it into his opponent's heart. The man slumped to the ground, unmoving, and Bergin turned to go, but before he could, a rough hand wrapped around his neck and held him tightly.

"Before I kill you," whispered a second barbarian, pressing a rusty dagger to the prince's throat, "I just want you to see this."

He yanked Bergin backwards and, still threatening him with the knife, gestured to the hill from where the Cordonians had attacked. But this time, instead of seeing his fellow countrymen, Bergin saw tens of thousands of the enemy, quietly crawling towards the city on their elbows and stomachs, obviously trying to remain unseen. Bergin's blood turned to ice. A sick, sick feeling spread throughout his stomach as he painfully realized that they had all just made a terrible, terrible mistake.

No wonder the barbarians had seemed so prepared for their attack! Because they had been! Somehow they had known about the Cordonians' plan and had decided to use it for their advantage! They had set a trap for them and now it seemed as if Bergin, Palo, and all the other brave men fighting today were going to pay the price.

"Like it?" asked the barbarian, digging the blade deeper into his victim's flesh. "Consider it a parting gift before you die."

Bergin swallowed.

"If I am to die," he said quietly, while forcing every ounce of fear out of his body, "at least I'll have died fighting for the greater good."

"Oh, not that nonsense again. You people, always talking about the gre—"

The sentence was never finished. The arm around Bergin's throat suddenly went slack and his would-be killer fell to the ground.

"Be a little more careful next time, brother dear," Palo said jokingly, while jerking his sword out of the dead man's body. "You had me worried there for a second."

He grinned and, at first, Bergin returned the smile. But then the full gravity of the situation hit and instantly the smile vanished.

"Palo," gasped Bergin, anxiety taking hold of him like a furious beast, "Palo, we have to get out of here! The barbarians! Somehow they knew about our surprise attack and now over a thousand more of them are coming from the north to trap us! We need to retreat before it's too late!"

Palo looked confused, so Bergin grabbed his head and turned it towards the direction of the hill, where the enemy was coming closer and closer to the city.

"No," whispered the heir, his face turning white. "No."

"Palo," Bergin urged again, this time in a shakier voice than before. "Palo, sound the retreat. Please, for the greater good, *sound the retreat*."

His brother needed no further encouragement. Trembling, Palo reached for the ivory horn at his side and was just about to blow it when an ear-piercing shriek cut through the air.

"Help!" screamed a voice, one that was low and cracked. "Somebody help me!"

Both princes turned to see a young Cordonian soldier several yards away from them, trapped against a wall and about to be killed by a large, angry-looking man with a spear.

Palo didn't hesitate. Grasping at the nearest thing available to him, the Crown Prince threw the horn at the barbarian's head as hard as he could and watched with satisfaction as it rammed against its target.

"No!" screamed Bergin, but it was too late.

The horn knocked the barbarian unconscious and toppled to the ground a second before he did. The Cordonian, utterly terrified, took off running, leaving the one thing they all needed to escape alone and out of reach in the dirt.

Palo's eyes widened in panic. He started moving forward to retrieve it, but, before he had even taken two steps, his entire body suddenly went rigid and he froze. Silent tears streamed down his cheeks and his face twisted in agony.

"Palo!" Bergin shouted, as his brother started swaying from side to side. "Palo, what's wrong with you!?"

Palo didn't answer him. Instead, he let out a low moan and then immediately crumpled to the ground, revealing a long, slender arrow jutting out from his calf as he fell. Bergin gasped. The arrow was probably a stray, but Bergin could tell from the purple liquid dripping from it that it was definitely poisoned.

He gritted his teeth. Poisons were a favorite of the barbarians and Bergin had no doubt that the one Palo was currently infected with was designed to kill, most likely within minutes. Of course, the antidote was fairly simple: just wash the wound in clean water for a few seconds and it would be healed. Easy. Yet at the same time entirely impossible.

Finding clean water in the middle of a city might not have been so hard, but finding water *and* regaining the horn? That was too much. That took time and Bergin simply didn't have that. His soldiers needed him. His *people* needed him. Palo may have put the life of one man above the lives of ten hundred others, but Bergin couldn't afford to make the same mistake. Those men *needed* to live another day because they needed to *fight* another day. But Palo ... Palo could be replaced. He could be replaced by Bergin.

Resolved, the prince turned from his brother's side and took off running towards the horn. He flew across the ground like a bird, sprinting faster than he ever had in his life, all so he could retrieve a thousand Cordonians' one chance at escaping from a certain death.

His heart burned with sadness as he ran and tears whipped across his face as he thought of Palo, rapidly dying on a freezing ground, maybe even dead already. But Bergin didn't let that stop him. He didn't let that cause him to turn around and search for water to heal his brother. He kept going. He had to.

He had to for the greater good.

Cities of the Gods

Ellen Pan

Grade 9. East High School, Lincoln, NE. Francesca Rohrs, Educator. *Honorable Mention.*

The Believer World

Gary looked up at the sky. It was turning a cloudy purple, swirls of dying red and curling blue smoke hugging its edges. The sky was a huge flower, he thought, and the sun was its pistil. In the morning the sun shed golden pollen and in the evening the flower died to be reborn the next morning.

His goats huddled in a pile under a large poplar tree, bleating as the last few rays of welcome sun melted into the horizon, and all became dark.

Gary's old blue eyes, diluted to a watery gray and well lined with the press of age, flickered through the thick scarf he was wearing over his head, scanning the grassy landscape for a village of some sorts. Right over a small wood not far from him was a bulb of golden light and shadows too sharp for nature thrown over the earth. Gary's stories were well known all over this part of the world; he would be recognized and welcomed at the village.

Giving a raspy cry, the old man, stooped with age and burdened with stories to tell, beckoned his unwilling goats up from their sleep and started for the village ahead of him.

....

"It's a raconteur!"

"Where? Where?"

"There, with his goats! A raconteur, with stories!"

The whole village came alive with people and bare feet speeding across the dusty paths. The crooked old man was instantly swarmed with laughing children and women hurrying forth to offer him food and drink.

A crackling fire was swiftly risen from dry logs, and before long its flames were licking the ink-black sky. Nearly the whole village had gathered around the roaring warmth, Gary in the midst of them all. Drunk on the finest wine offered by the villagers, he was a bit dizzy and confused, and the glowing red warmth on his weathered face threatened to seal his eyes with dream-filled sleep. Still, he put away the wish and opened his mouth to tell another story in return for the villagers' warm welcome and gifts.

"Far up in the sky, past the height of fluffy white clouds and glittering stars, there stands a kingdom with the name of Harrelore, filled with the strangest creatures that never come down to roam the lands of the

Earth. The Cities of the Gods are all up in that kingdom, of course. There are gods that control rain and thunder, gods that control the harvest in the fall, and ones that create chaos, war, and strength. The gods that rule our land, they're all up there in the sky. When we worship them, they are the strongest; when no raconteur is left to tell the stories of a god, that god would fade away as their believers dwindle and disappear altogether when he is forgotten at last."

The children's faces were stretched with eagerness, their features dancing in the flickering firelight.

Gary continued, barely able to keep his eyes open. "But there's one thing about Harrelore that's the queerest ... everything there, it's all upside down. Children run with their feet glued to the sky, and castles are built with their turrets pointing down. Some sailors say that they once saw a gleaming red roof peek through the folds of clouds when they were on the swaying ocean."

He cleared his throat, attempting to keep his gaze in focus. The honeyed wine was so lulling, so sweet, that he could no longer decipher what was real and what was not. "Tonight, I will tell you about a new god—of Harrelore—a god of grace that brings dance and song—!"

The shapes before the fire were swimming together into a fuzzy blob now, but Gary managed to open his mouth and speak once more.

....

Gary opened his eyes to a buttery ray of sunlight peeking in between the curtains and a strange bed under him. Still groggy from wine, the old raconteur sat up.

A few children were playing at his door when he went outside to greet the sunlight.

"Thank you for the story last night, Gary!"

"We love Nusp!"

Gary didn't know of anyone named Nusp. He walked through all the thousands of stories he'd told in the past but came up with nothing.

Before Gary could question the boys further, a woman's voice called his name down the street. She was herding his goats with a branch and holding his bags in the other hand. He bid goodbye to the boys and hurried to collect his things.

What Gary didn't remember about the other night, when his head was swollen with wine, was a grave mistake that he had made in his myth. Rather than a beautiful god of grace with an enchanting name, he had created a foul peasant that was displeasing in every way, save for his amazing ability at dancing and singing. Nusp was this god's name—one that Gary would never have dreamt up if he had been any more sensible.

But of course Gary the raconteur knew nothing of this, and he had no intention to change anything he spoke of that night at the village.

The Myth World

Nusp, on the other hand, was not having such a good time on the island of Harrelore. He had opened his eyes standing in the right place—the floating palace of the gods, a place where everything was lavished with marble and gold. He himself, however, was very far from matching this palace's splendor. A head like a potato sat upon Nusp's long neck, and graceful, muscled limbs hung from his twisted torso like some sort of mistake. Apart from his strange appearance, Nusp could also have easily been the dirtiest man on earth.

It went without saying that Nusp was brutally thrown from the palace in the sky, his spot among the ivory thrones denied. Alone, confused, and revolted by everyone else, this wretched god of grace hid himself between the darkest crevices of the Twin Giants, brother mountains that stood taller than the clouds, guarding the island of Harrelore.

Immortal as he was, Nusp lived in his lightless recluse for over two million sunrises and sunsets. His clear voice was his one companion, ringing throughout the steep, black mountains; later generations of islanders who knew not of Nusp thought that it was the Twin Giants that sung to them. Nusp danced alone in his cave, stunning twirls and leaps never kissed by the gift of daylight; in this dark crevice he stayed for a long time, but no secret could be kept forever.

"Be gone, you foul creature!"

A crew of men had finally decided to venture into the Twin Giants that day, determined to uncover the true identity of this singing angel. What they found when they reached the source of song, however, was far from their expectations. Where they hoped to find a long-lost nymph, their flickering torchlight shined straight upon Nusp's misshapen face. Two million days without showering had made him horrendous to look at. The men gave Nusp no time to explain himself with their continuous use of projectile weaponry, and so the great, wretched god ran away into the depths of the mountains. Soon enough, hundreds of men, women, and children had abandoned their tasks and ventured down the narrow paths that Nusp took.

Deep within the dark, Nusp buried his hideous face in his hands. "Oh, what am I supposed to do?" he sobbed to himself in the musical voice that had brought all the trouble. "Curse the raconteur who breathed me to life with his wretched words—I don't blame them for despising a beast as ugly as I!"

There was no other way of escape from the jabbing words and abuse. Two million sunrises and sunsets Nusp had suffered their wrath, and now it was time to retreat to the part of the world that none of the villagers could reach.

Extending his long, godly arms, Nusp pulled himself high up onto the steep, black bones of the Twin Giants, stretched himself to all his grace, and climbed to the peak of the snowy mountain. It took the god eight whole days, but those days held the promise of peace.

Finally at the snow-capped peaks, sitting above the ears of the Twin Giants, Nusp could hear the squabbling voices of peasants still searching for his shadow, craving his blood far below on the ground, but he was far from their reach. Here, Nusp was safe—for a while, at least. What he didn't know, or rather, what nobody knew was that something called *science* was growing in the Believer world down below. As science prospered, myths started to fade and become forgotten. Small things disappeared at first, one at a time—a witch today, a vampire tomorrow. But the end of Harrelore was soon to come.

The Believer World

The world was shaken when the first periodic table of elements was drawn with quaking lines in 1869. Before this, no one knew or even dreamt that the world was built out of countless tiny particles that the sharpest eye could not see.

There were so many scientific discoveries in that period of time. People learned that the air wasn't *nothing*, but a mixture of gases; they learned that rain and thunder were created by winds and waves, not the anger of a god.

By the time the 20th century rolled around, few people remembered the tale of a red roof poking down from the sky many centuries ago. Gary and his fellow raconteurs had long entered the doors of death; no one spoke of the Cities of the Gods.

Science was such a fabulous thing, everyone marveled. Everything makes so much more sense now.

But for those up high in the lands of Harrelore, where the gods dwelled on belief, things were quite the contrary right now.

The Myth World

Even from the height that Nusp sat, he could tell that something was terribly wrong in Harrelore. He could feel himself fading away, his very existence blurring with fewer and fewer believers. Some days he woke up unable to remember his own name and other days missing entire chunks of his past.

Today was extremely terrible. Nusp could feel his very being flickering in and out of focus, like he was going to disintegrate into nothingness any second.

For over three million sunrises and sunsets Harrelore had stood its ground in the sky. Nusp thought. Was it truly at its demise now? What of the raconteurs that told the stories of the gods?

A deep rumbling came from underneath him. Looking down, Nusp saw with alarm that the Twin Giants themselves were trembling like volcanoes ready to erupt. Great chunks of their black bones rolled off the edge, shattered into dust and nothing more in midair. Could it be—

Before he had the time to think things through, Nusp leapt as far as he could into the air, his fingers reaching wildly for the tall, blue expanse that was supposedly his sky and the believers' sea. If this was true, then—

In midair, Nusp felt a wave of nausea as up became down and down became up, and he plummeted fast, fast into the Believer world as Harrelore, home to the Cities of Gods, shook in its wake. Behind him, the two great guardians of his homeland exploded in unison into great clouds of dust, carried away by the winds and gone forever.

The Believer World

One day near the end of summer, a man fell from the sky.

The sailors passing by on a ship saw him fall. He descended from the clouds, flailing, and dove straight into the ocean. Surprised, they stopped the ship and went for a closer look.

At first, the sailors weren't sure that what they were seeing was a man. He was at least ten feet in height, with yellow matted hair so greasy that droplets of water rolled right off the strands. Everyone aboard was utterly speechless at the sudden arrival. He certainly didn't look like an angel, and in the seawater there was an almost definite sheen of oil in a ring all around him.

The sailors threw the strange creature a lifesaver and watched him, spluttering, clamber up. Now in full view, everyone was secretly glad that he had taken a dunk in the water before getting on the ship. Still there was an impressive amount of grime stuck to his skin like leeches.

The sailors asked the strange man who he was and where he was from. They pelted him with questions, but all they received was his name, Nusp.

"Nusp? What kind of name is that?"

This time, there was no response save for the gagged coughing of the bent creature.

"Let's get you to our next destination." The crew finally decided after a long, fruitless attempt at making conversation. "That's America. Ever heard of the place? It's a great country. I'm sure the people there will be able to help you find your way home."

I hope so, Nusp thought silently. But he said nothing more as the ship cut white slices through the waves, headed into the unknown.

....

Nusp wasn't sure what to make of this America when he set foot on its soil. Tall, sharp buildings stood like glaring soldiers in every place, and strange metal creatures ran like the wind on four wheels as they spluttered with groans. He saw too many things here that he had never dreamt of before, including a box that could show him anything in the world with the press of a button. Nusp thought that it was far more reliable than a magic orb.

He slowly learned the customs of this strange new world. He learned that the time was counted by years, and that he was living in the 1957th one; he learned to make a living on the streets by sharing his breathtaking voice and dance to the world. In the Believer world, his gnarled face didn't seem to matter as long as he had talent to display. Nusp was soon recruited to be an acrobat and singer in the circus and travelled to other parts of the world with nothing but his voice and his graceful limbs to support him.

Nusp had been reassured by many people in America that there were no such things as gods and that Harrelore must have been nothing more than a vivid dream. Indeed there were no gods here, no one who wielded the power to create lightning, thunder, or bloody war, but in the Believer world, Nusp felt more like a god than he had ever felt in Harrelore, millions of days ago. He enjoyed the spotlight in the middle of the stage each time the circus put up a performance, and he loved flying through the air with his limbs extended, one with the sky. Still, something was missing from his life. To Nusp, the Believer world was built out of nothing but precise calculations, of machines that worked not by belief and hope but by the push and pull of levers. Nusp still longed to return where he was originally born and belonged. But the Myth world, he knew, was shattered from head to toe since he descended into the Believer world—unless there was a way to bring it back.

....

Nusp looked up at the sky. It was turning a cloudy purple, swirls of dying red and curling blue smoke hugging its edges. The sky was a huge flower, he thought, and the sun was its pistil. In the morning, the sun shed golden pollen and in the evening, the flower died to be reborn the next morning.

The rest of the circus huddled in a pile under a large poplar tree as the last few rays of welcome sun melted into the horizon, and all became dark. Nusp swiftly lit a giant campfire out in the clearing and beckoned everyone to sit around. In the flickering fire light, their expressions danced, stretched with eagerness. Nusp took a deep breath and began to speak.

"Far up in the sky, past the height of fluffy white clouds and glittering stars, there stands a kingdom with the name of Harrelore, filled with the strangest creatures that never come down to roam the lands of the Earth ..."

For days he went on, racking his memories of all that he knew about his native land. As the circus travelled over the world, Nusp spread his stories along with him. The Myth world began to recreate itself, bit by bit, as the stories started to flow again. The number of believers rose and dipped with time until the stories passed into the ears of a young girl the age of 14, who decided to turn all of this into a story.

That young girl was me, and the story is what's before your eyes this very moment. The Myth world was preserved at its peak through black ink on white paper, never to cease even if no one else remembered the existence of Harrelore. More young writers learned about the Cities of Gods through writing and added color of their own until the legends were once more thriving up high beyond folds of white clouds.

And what happened to Nusp, you may ask? Well, he flew in an airplane back to the spot that he fell from, entered the clouds and was never seen again. I know that he's back in Harrelore now, the place where he belonged, this time with an ivory throne of his own in the palace of the gods. Often times, other people from the Believer world travelled to the Myth world as well, in airplanes and ships, and they have yet to return—for the place that Nusp descended from, its name is now the Bermuda Triangle.

Model Minority

Clarissa Tan

Grade 10. East High School, Lincoln, NE. Sarah Staples-Farmer, Educator. *Gold Key.*

critical essay

Asian without "A"s spells "sin"; we are nothing without good grades and academic prowess. The model minority, "studious Asian" stereotype ignores all our individuality and uniquenesses. We are socially categorized and considered identical before others even get to know us. I've been told "all Asians are the same" more times than I can count; we have the same straight black hair, the same small eyes and flat features, and the same "perfect" genius brain. Every Asian can play the piano at its perfection with one hand tied behind their back and there is no math problem in the world an Asian can't solve. Our achievements are insignificant and go unacknowledged because success has become a given. The term "model minority" seeks to render our discrimination invisible by implying we face no racial injustices. But in reality, Asians must endure severe prejudices egged on by racialization and stereotypical assumptions.

At my elementary school, Asians were rare. Whenever we learned about China or anything remotely "un-American," I felt the eyes of everyone on my back as if I were suddenly thrust into a great spotlight. But as a young girl I had no method of coping; I was one of four total Asians at school. I thought it normal for women of color to be treated differently and excluded from social activities. I felt ashamed of myself because I didn't look like the other kids. I was ashamed of speaking Chinese in front of them. I was ashamed of my "squinty eyes" and "yellow skin."

As I grew older, I learned that those hurtful comments were not just youthful ignorance. It was routine for Asians to experience racism, which we must learn to deal with if we are to survive in this world. However, racism and stereotyping had extended to a point where they affected my daily life and actions. People piled enormous amounts of pressure on me, and the expectation to be perfect grew higher and higher each year. Getting a 98 is unsatisfying and never enough, because it could have been 100. For many Asians, there are minimal breaks from the constant pain of work. Instead of playing outside with the other kids, the Asians I knew were slumped over math books at the dinner table. If we don't win a math competition or go to science bowl nationals, which are stereotypically "Asian" activities, we are deemed failures who will have no future. While many attempt to escape the status quo, we may be eventually bogged down by the societal beliefs dumped on

critical essay

us. Asians have been raised with the idea that we are naturally gifted and that we must excel in all fields, such as being the next Beethoven. That is the only life we have known.

Eventually, I, with many others, started buying into the belief that academic success is the only way forward. Getting into an Ivy League college would gain approval from family and the Asian community, who all work tirelessly as lawyers or doctors. The possibility of failing would undermine all their efforts. As a result, most Asians spend their entire high school careers preparing for college admission, which revolves around gathering trophies. The model minority assumption sets impossibly high standards, yet we Asians must keep reaching for them. No matter how persistently we work, it is never enough because we're constantly preoccupied about missing out on potential opportunities. Race alone has devalued our efforts, which are treated as nothing when they cost us considerable amounts of time and energy. There's no time for "fun and enjoyment" when we could be grinding for Harvard. After all, who wants to become the "family disappointment"?

Despite all this, I agree with the correctness of the model minority. Life doesn't lie; it is indeed true many Asians excel socioeconomically. However, because of the stereotype, our talents and achievements are overlooked and considered "the norm." But that is what

"Asian" is. After all, what power do we wield without a perfect GPA? All the hard work poured into our studies is nothing due to the nonchalant "Asian genes" theory. Everything we do is inevitably attributed to race, and, no matter how much everyone tries to dilute it, there is forever an underlying hint of judgement. People think our achievements were easily obtained and fail to consider the sacrifices made on our part. All of the effort and dedication to earn "impressive" results are simply swept aside.

Yet, the model minority stereotype causes even more harm to the Asians struggling in their academics. They are afraid of asking for help, even after repeatedly being told "it's all right." We all know that look—a slight part of the lips and a quick raise of the brow, so fast and light barely anyone would notice. That flash of surprise discourages the confused from seeking help, because they feel all Asians are smart and should require no assistance in their studies. In freshman year, I found out I had received a B+ on a math test, which led to noises of shock from my classmates and a suggestion to go to the "learning hub." They simply could not handle the fact that I was anything below an "A" student. No matter the subject or our skill level, everyone expects us to have it mastered. Of course, the "learning hub" is never a viable solution for Asians. Receiving help would mean accepting defeat, which comes with a boatload of judgement and embarrassment. If one just does not fit into the all-successful, whiz-kid myth, they do not have a place in society.

What is my power against all the hidden skepticism? I tell myself as long as I am still living and breathing, there is no reason for me not to be able to push through another day. Resilience is strength, like a fist to haul me through all the milestones of life. I wake every morning worrying about SAT scores, grades, upcoming competitions, and other Asian responsibilities. The idea of failing keeps me moving forth, to stand strong among the discrimination thrown at me from all sides, even if their origins were innocuous. Life is not easy for a woman of color, but I know I am not alone. 2.25 billion other Asian women stand with me on this planet, and purely choosing to exist in a society that stands silently against us is my weapon of choice.

critical essay

When a Pitiful Creature Becomes an Abusive Monster

Malik Gillespie

Grade 12. Westside High School, Omaha, NE. Liz Hough, Dana Rose, Educators. *Silver Key.*

Portfolio Silver Key

When it comes to Mary Shelley's seminal and famous novel *Frankenstein,* the mastery that she displays of written literature allows for an incredible amount of ideas to be fit onto her pages: the dynamic relationship between "creator" and "creation"; what it means to be moral; nature's triumph over humanity's unnatural creations (mis)using science; the idea of monstrosity and humanity with the question of "what makes someone a monster"; and so many more themes and ideas all weaved together to create the compelling story that is considered to be the foundational text of the entire genre of science fiction. While the topic that I chose to talk about is neither obscure and minuscule nor well known and surface-level, the topic of abuse and the effects of trauma and abandonment is an incredibly complex concept in reality—one that Shelley does not attempt to simplify in any way—and it converges with every other major theme in her book.

It's important to note that trauma and abuse are not topics to be taken lightly, and I do not believe that Shelley is doing so in her novel; in fact, I believe she does the opposite in how she constructed her antagonist (I hesitate to truly call him a villain, which is a testament to the quality of her writing) in the Creature who is so human in how he adopts the abusive behavior of Victor, the man who fills the role of "father." Victor himself is consistently portrayed as self-centered and egotistical, which is displayed in multiple parts throughout the book, but I believe it is best encapsulated in the scene in which Victor truly transitions from a tragically flawed protagonist to an irredeemable man, where he too transitions into a monster. Just after the Creature frames Justine, a woman who was apparently a very close friend of Victor's family, for the murder of his younger brother, something Victor *knows* to be untrue, the woman comes to accept her death sentence. In response to learning this information, Shelley writes Victor's inner monologue to say, "The tortures of the accused did not equal mine; she was sustained by innocence, but the fangs of remorse tore my bosom and would not forgo their hold ... I cannot pretend to describe what I felt. I had before experienced sensations of horror ... but words cannot convey an idea of the heart-sickening despair that I endured" (69–70). To put aside the argument of whether Victor truly is psychologically suffering more than Justine because it's irrelevant right now, the point here is Victor's response to hearing the testimony of a person he *knows* is innocent accepting the punishment of death when he has the power to—and, some would argue, responsibility to—speak up on her behalf. It isn't even that he didn't admit his mistake of creating the Creature that actually did the murder; the crux of what makes this act irredeemable is that Victor compares himself to Justine and concludes that he is indeed suffering more than she is right now, instead of having compassion for her situation or trying to comfort her in any way or any number of other ways that he could put the needs of a desperate person above his own. This lack of compassion and self-awareness while simultaneously desiring social acceptance from the people he doesn't see as equals is what drives him to reject and abandon the Creature and keep it a secret.

Shelley describes the moment of Victor's rejection relatively early on in the book (from Victor's perspective, at least), writing, "His jaws opened, and he muttered some inarticulate sounds, while a grin wrinkled his cheeks. He might have spoken, but I did not hear; one hand was stretched out, seemingly to detain me, but I escaped and rushed downstairs" (43). While this is an understandable reaction, it's important to keep in mind that abusers may not know that they are or even mean to act abusive or be perpetrators of another person's abuse; regardless, Victor actively rejecting what is, in essence, a newborn and running away is an act of abuse.

It is very clear in the book that Victor abandoning the Creature immediately after his experiment and creation of life is the event that the Creature uses to justify his anger at Victor. During the confrontation between Victor and the Creature on the mountain where the creature shares his story, he says, "I was benevolent and good; misery made me a fiend. Make me happy, and I shall again be virtuous" (Shelley 84). The Creature, like all newborns, was an innocent at the beginning of his life, and he blames the pain of abandonment and suffering of rejection on why he's a monster.

Before I continue, I want to make clear that I am not going to deny that those who face social rejection and deal with the psychologically damaging effects of it have the possibility of beginning to engage in malevolent actions or behaviors seen as immoral, that the abused have the possibility of becoming abusers. With that being made clear, the reasoning of the Creature is wrong. I agree that the monster is justified in his anger at Victor; what he is not justified in doing is blaming Victor for becoming a true monster, for becoming an abuser. It was his own actions that made him a monster;

the Creature chose to become a monster when he chose to act exactly how everyone thought he would and feared him for. The Creature became a monster when he chose to act like Victor and when he chose to terrorize and lash out at people. This is not saying that Victor and society are completely innocent, of course. I simply cannot accept the Creature's justification for his actions, that it is because of how he was treated by Victor and the world his entire short life that he's grotesque in both body and soul now. To quote the freelance writer and essayist Ian Danskin, "That is the broken narrative spit from the lips of a hundred thousand broken people. People who say 'it's not me, it's just this awful world'; people who say, 'if you'd lived my life, you'd probably be the same' ... They say it's not their fault ... While trauma may be used by abusive people to justify being more abusive, the one does not create the other where it didn't already exist."

This added subtext of Victor and the Creature both being abusive monsters, specifically to each other, poses a question that is fitting of the complexity of both the entire issue of trauma and abuse as well as Mary Shelley's entire novel, but I think is somewhat surface level with this perspective: who is more abusive? In my opinion, however, the better question that is implicitly asked is do these monsters deserve sympathy? That is a much more loaded question.

Not That Simple

Jayden Leonard

Grade 12. Thayer Central High School, Hebron, NE. Anne Heitmann, Educator. *Honorable Mention.*

critical essay

In the 2016 film *I Am Not Your Negro*, directed by Raoul Peck, the writings of James Baldwin and clips of his speeches are used to inform viewers about the lives of Medgar Evers, Malcolm X, and Martin Luther King, Jr., and how they affected each other in order to influence our view on the state of African Americans today. The documentary is split into sections corresponding with stages of Baldwin's life and his different struggles with racial issues.

In the first section, "Paying My Dues," Baldwin is drawn to return to America after seeing newspaper stories about Dorothy Counts. He states that he didn't miss anything that represented America, but he missed his people.

The second section, "Heroes," discusses people who shaped Baldwin's point of view. He talks of his white schoolteacher, black actors who portrayed their realities accurately, and his thoughts about how white actors who do awful things in their movies are made out to be heroes.

In the third section, "Witness," he tells about his encounters with the three men, and in the fourth section, "Purity," Baldwin says that the treatment of black people was partially a result of white people trying to purify themselves.

In the fifth section, "Selling the Negro," he discusses the issue that an uninformed America is in having people support the cause for equality.

The sixth and last section, "I Am Not a 'N-word,'" ends with a monologue from Baldwin where he challenges the American people to ask themselves why they needed that word in the first place (Peck).

This is a hard-hitting documentary which uses parts of James Baldwin's interviews, real-life footage, and movie clips to accurately portray the racial issues in this country and discuss their roots. I strongly agree with a number of the statements that Baldwin made throughout the film, but I don't agree with his idealistic view on how to solve the problem of racism.

"If I am not the "n-word" here and you invented him, you the white people invented him, then you've got to find out why. And the future of the country depends on that, whether or not it is able to ask that question" (Baldwin 109). In *I Am Not Your Negro,* a documentary directed by Raoul Peck, James Baldwin is quoted saying this. Throughout the film, clips of Baldwin's interviews and his narrated writings are used to persuade us to agree with his view of the state of African Americans in this country. Two of his statements that I agree fully with involve the ideas of "American blindness" and white power; however, based on the reality of these two social constructs, I don't agree with Baldwin's idealistic solution quoted previously.

The notion of American blindness is touched on throughout the film. Simply stated, this means that we think that being American makes us better. This is exemplified regularly in the film by the short movie clips of the "perfect" American life. They show how we liked to view America: pretty ladies, white picket fences, the land of equal opportunity. The reason I agree so strongly that this is how we perceived America is because this is how a lot of us still view life here today. We see America as the land of the free and the home of the brave. We take pride in our strong morals and founding values. But has America always been the "land of the free" or even "the brave"? One of our founding principles was that all men are created equal. If we really believed that was true, why would we have had the issue of slavery and racism in the first place? In the fifth section, "Selling the Negro," James Baldwin writes, "chief among them that American blindness, or cowardice which allows us to pretend that life presents no reasons for being bitter" (98). In addition to only seeing America as a country far ahead of all the others, we also are blind to the bad things that are going on and have gone on in this country. Included in the film to contrast the clips of old movies was recent news footage of riots and racial violence. Many Americans missed seeing these stories in the news, and I have no doubt that there were people in the time of Baldwin who had no idea how African American people were really being treated.

The second idea that I think is still prevalent in our world view today is white supremacy. At the beginning of the last section, "I Am Not a 'N-word,'" Baldwin writes, "I attest to this: the world is not white; it never was white, cannot be white. White is a metaphor for power" (107). Something I don't understand is if people with darker skin have practically always been around, why did we ever get the idea that being white made us automatically better? Even if we don't actually believe this, we've been conditioned to have presumptions about the nature of a white person's character compared to that of an African American. If we were faced with two people, one white and one black, who were suspects for a crime, we would automatically assume that the black man is guilty. The idea that white men are supposed to be the "good guys" has been instilled in us since we can remember. In the documentary clips white "heroes" are shown unjustly chasing Native Americans off of their land. Watching scenes like these makes me feel guilty although I personally had no say or part in the awful things that our ancestors did. Something that most people need to realize is that we are not our race; we are not the people who came before us. We should not continue to think we are entitled to certain things because we are white; this makes us no different than the Europeans who first settled this country.

I believe James Baldwin had an acute grasp on the human condition, but I do not agree that simply asking ourselves why would change anything. In his monologue at the end of the film, Baldwin says, "What white people have to do is try and find out in their own hearts why it was necessary to have a 'n-word' in the first place" (109). I would argue that this solution is too idealistic and temporary. I think some people would consider this question, yes, but others would ignore it. Some people are incapable of thinking deeply or concerning themselves with such issues. Society has always found a way to oppress a group of people, no matter what set them apart: the Jews in Europe, the Native Americans in this country, African Americans in our past and present, unborn children now. This is something I don't believe will stop by simply asking why we do it. We will continue to dehumanize groups of people no matter how we advance in other areas of life. As for an actual solution, it isn't so simple to say there's only one approach we could take to change everything. So, while I don't agree fully with Baldwin, I also don't think any of the men whose lives he observed had the right idea on their own either. I think the reason that we've made progress is because of the variety of positions that these leaders did take. People were bound to follow at least one of them.

The reality of "American blindness" and white power causes James Baldwin's solution of self-reflection to be unreasonable. I enjoyed the documentary, and it definitely made me think more deeply about these issues. Although I would also like to be an optimist like Baldwin, I have come to the conclusion that there will always be some people who are unaware of what's going on around them and we will always have the need to be superior to someone else. If we really want to change the way we treat people who are different or oppressed, we should be asking ourselves how, not why, and then actually make the change.

The Private Investigator

Landon Boettcher

Grade 10. Franklin Public School, Franklin, NE. Adam Boettcher, Educator. *Honorable Mention.*

novel writing

Brief Summary

Retired from his time with the undercover agency of the gunsluggers, an alien hunting team of men and women different from the others, Tom Neilson becomes Corner Cove's top private investigator, and, as his first investigation, he has to find out what has happened to his beloved old friend, Carl Jubber. In doing so, he finds not only that Carl is still alive but that an alien race thought to have been extinct years ago known as the Zardons have been thriving inside one of the old agents. It is now up to Tom, Carl, and some of their old friends to stop the Zardonian Invasion. Meanwhile, in an alternate world, Falcon Howlette and Halo must stop a demonic invasion that wants to merge the five realms into one, and a young teen by the name of Gregory Michaels finds out his father has been transported there by accident and must find out what happened to his father as well as if Tom Neilson will help him. All havoc comes to an end that comes up as wild, mysterious, and straight-up crazy. The town of Corner Cove wouldn't be the same if it wasn't for one private investigator who just wanted to live his life as a normal human for a couple of years. Five realms, a team of supernatural investigators, worlds of furies, angels, and demons, and one action can change the outcome of the entire world ... no pressure!

Excerpt

I

It was a cold night and Carl Jubber was walking home from his recent viewing of the new *Galaxy Adventure* movie. Carl looks up at the stars, each one twinkling with delight, then he looks back at his path, bumping into a tall, dark figure. "Oops, I am so sorry," Carl said to the figure. "I didn't see you there!" The figure turns to Carl and snarls at his witty personality.

"Don't you know who I am?" the figure asked.

Carl thought long and hard on his answer, but he eventually came up with this answer: "Did we go to college together?"

"College?" the figure bellowed. "Hah! I never went to college and I never will! I am the strongest, smartest man alive!"

Carl thought deeply about the clues the figure gave him and said, "Bill Gates? No ... Elon Musk? No, that's not it ... Doctor Emmet Brown!"

The figure stares at Carl with disbelief. "You really don't know who I am, do you?" Carl just shakes his head. The figure sighed. "Fine, might as well be on your way, then." But before Carl could take a step, the figure pulls out a metal arm holding a pistol, black and well-shaped. Carl suddenly puts up his hands and freezes in the sight of this awesome weapon. "Everyone knows who I am," the figure explained. "And if you don't, you're obviously an imposter!"

"Wait!" Carl shouted without question. "That voice sounds familiar!"

"Shut up!" the figure shouted back. "You're just saying that so I don't shoot you!"

"No, no, really! Your voice sounds like Jerry," Carl explained.

"Jerry? Who the blooming heck is Jerry?" the figure asked.

"My nephew!" The figure rolls his eyes and shoots the poor man. Carl slumped down to his knees, uttering the words, "Jerry, why?" and falls to his death.

The figure steps up to the now dead Carl Jubber and tells the corpse, "I am not Jerry."

Three days later, Carl's wife, Janis, is weeping in front of the town of Corner Cove's best private investigator, Thomas Edwin Neilson. "I don't know where he is," Janis wept. "I looked everywhere, even the theater! Oh, Thomas, please, please help me find my husband!"

Tom looks at Janis, her eyes full of wet, salty tears. He then looks at a framed photo of his wife, Anna, on his desk, then back at Janis. "Okay, I'll help you find your husband," he finally says, "if you give me a price."

"Any price! I've got the cash! If you'd—"

"No cash," Tom insisted, "just a baker's dozen of chocolate doughnuts."

"Well, in that case, I'll make them homemade! As long as you find my husband!" Janis told him. Tom tells her they have a deal and they shake on that deal. Thirteen doughnuts for the investigation on the missing husband, Carl Jubber.

II

Later that night, Tom walks into the dining room to see his wife setting the table. Anna finally sits down in front of her plate as Tom sits next to her, setting his investigating notebook beside him. Anna looks over and stares at the notebook, filled with Post It notes marking certain sections. "Another case?" Anna asked.

"Nothing like lost car keys this time, Anna," Tom said.

"Lost puppy?" Anna hoped.

"Nope," Tom said. "This time, it's a real case. A person is missing!"

"Hey! Dogs are people, too!" Anna argued.

Tom stared at his wife, smiled with reassurance, and told her, "Yeah, sure, honey."

"Who's missing?"

"Carl Jubber."

"The neighbor?"

"Yup, the neighbor." Tom fiddled with his food as he chewed on a piece of fat.

"Oh my gosh!" Anna exclaimed. "Janis must be devastated!"

"She was," Tom told her. "I'm pretty sure she still is. Thanks for the food, by the way." Tom got up and put his plate away.

"Well, I am your wife!"

"You are?"

"Did you forget?"

"Forget what?"

"I am your wife, Tom!" Anna yelled, putting down her fork.

"Oh, yeah," Tom said. "Listen, I'm just really focused on this case."

"Okay." Anna calmed herself and gave her husband a reassuring smile. "Good luck, Tom." Anna gets up, walks in front of her love and kisses him. Tom thanks her, leaving for bed that night.

The next day, Tom inspects the crime scene in which Carl Jubber was supposedly last seen: the alleyway near the theater. He sees blood on the ground, dried from the four days since Carl's disappearance. Tom looks up to relax his neck and sees a young boy, roughly eighteen, taking out the trash, but when he opened the garbage lid, he jumped with fear. His bag fell onto the ground, and so did he. Tom rushed over to aid the boy and hopefully get some questions answered. "Kid, do you mind if I ask you a couple questions?" Tom paused hovering over the boy. The boy didn't say a word. "I'll take that as a 'yes.' Now, were you present the night Carl Jubber got kidnapped about four days ago?" The boy just stares at the private investigator. "Kid?" Tom reassured the kid was still alive by snapping about his face. The kid blinked a couple times. "What's the matter? What happened?" The boy points to the garbage, its lid still open. "I know, it stinks, can you just focus?"

"It ... it's a man!" the boy managed, failing to get himself up off the ground. Confused, Tom walks over to the garbage and peeks inside. Sure enough, there was a man in there, with blood across his chest.

"Dang it!" Tom shouted, slamming his palms on the edge of the garbage. He turns to look at the boy. "Thank you for your time." He walks for a couple feet, then sprints head long toward home to tell his wife the bad news.

When he got there, Janis was in the kitchen with Anna, and conveniently so. They were baking doughnuts for Tom's case, and Tom had just ruined the surprise ingredient: *frosting*. "I mean, of course Tom would ask you to bake these. They're his favorite!" Anna exclaimed.

"I'd do anything to get my husband back," Janis said, walking over to wash her hands.

"I suppose anyone would. Are you sure you're fine, Janis?" Anna asked in reassurance.

"Yes, I'm fine," Janis said. "Just get off my back about it, will you? Tom has it covered! He is Corner Cove's greatest private investigator, after all."

Just then Anna notices her husband's presence. Tom was sweating and had fear about his eyes. He panted like there was no tomorrow. "Tom! What happened?" Anna finally asked.

"Did you find my husband?" Janis continued.

Tom looks at Janis, then back at Anna. He is now about in tears, but, before he breaks, he hugs Anna. "Tom, what's going on?" Anna asked, feeling as if everything may not be okay.

Tom looks up at Janis, then whispers the words into Anna's ear, "Carl is dead." Anna gasped and walked back to comfort Janis.

"Thomas," Janis asked, "where's Carl?"

Anna begins to cry upon Janis's back as she managed to say the words, but it ended up sounding like "car-your-de." Janis somehow understood the message and fell to the floor, weeping in tears of grief.

III

Night fell and the moon shone on Carl's gravestone. Tom, Anna, and Janis surround the grave as they mourn for the loss of a dear friend and husband. The gravestone read: *In Loving Memory of one Carl Jubber, a dear friend to all, but an even better husband. 1985–2022.* Tom felt conflicted. He wanted to complete the case, though the case he's been assigned had already been completed: he found Carl. But there was something left untouched. Something was missing from the entire story. *How did Carl die?* And *who killed Carl Jubber?* Tom pondered this on his drive to his office. When he finally arrived, he sat at his desk, grabbed a doughnut, and thought long and hard on the little evidence he had found and whether or not he should find out the mystery. A knock on the door interrupted his train of thought. "Come in," Tom shouted. A man walked through the door, his mustache thin and his eyebrows thick. He walked up to the desk, seeing Tom continue his decision.

"Hey, buddy," the man said.

Tom looked up to see that man, who looked like he didn't shower in under thirty minutes. "James?" Tom said. "You're back from Mexico!"

"Yeah, just got back," James replied. "Figured I had to come visit the guy who found my car keys in Jellyzburg. How's business?"

"I was just in the middle of a murder case," Tom explained. "Carl Jubber, husband of Janis Jubber. I'm trying to decide whether or not I should find out who killed him or just leave the case as it is."

"Well, you definitely should!" James said. "You are a detective, aren't you?"

"Private investigator," Tom corrected.

"Sorry, P.I. Same difference, anyway," James said. "Who's the first suspect?"

"There was this boy working at the theater. He's the one who found the body," Tom said. "That's about all I know that may have seen him from that night."

James looks on Tom's desk. There was a peculiar file sticking underneath the Jubber file. James pulls it out and looks through it. "How did Carl die?"

"From what it appears, a gunshot to the heart," Tom answered. "Why?"

"Well, it says here, this guy named Jared Mow ... Mou ... something .... Jared is the only known gunslugger to live in Corner Cove," James replied. "It says here he lives up in Jellyzburg!"

novel writing

"Jared Moututou? I wouldn't think he'd come back just to kill a man," Tom pointed out.

"It's worth a visit," James said. "You know how gun-sluggers are. You were one, if I remember correctly."

Tom stared at his old friend and stood up. He looked at the framed photo of his wife and sighed. "Let's go to Jellyzburg." It took twenty minutes to get from Corner Cove to Jellyzburg, and both Tom and James got out of the car to walk up to the address at which the file had said Jared lived. James rang the doorbell and that made the wait an extra four minutes longer. Jared finally arrived at the door.

"What can I do for you, boys?" Jared asked. He was in his underwear, a robe covering his torso and waist. His feet were covered with socks: one long, one short. Jared's hair was long, his beard hung low, and his belly was out.

"Jared Moututou? I'm Tom Neilson, private investigator, and this is my old partner, James Paddens," Tom started. "We're here to ask you a few questions regarding the recent murder of Carl Jubber."

"Who the blooming heck is Carl Jubber?" Jared bellowed, drinking from a bottle he had in his prosthetic hand.

"We just want answers, Jared, not harm," James assured the man.

"Well, sorry, boys, but I have no idea who this man is," Jared said, closing his door. James stopped the door with his foot.

"We just need a moment of your time," James said.

"Are you calling me a liar?" Jared bellowed.

"Come on, James, he clearly doesn't know what you're talking about. Let's just head back to the office and—" Tom began.

"No, no, we're here to ask questions, and we deserve answers!" James exclaimed.

"I'm going to sue you if you don't get off my property in the next seven minutes!" Jared yelled.

"Oh, please!" James scoffed. "You don't have the money!"

"Don't you know who I am?"

"Mow ... mou ..." James stuttered.

"Moututou, Jared Moututou, officer in command from the recently disbanded gunsluggers," Tom said.

"You got further than the one guy I bumped into in Corner Cove!" Jared exclaimed. They all pause for a brief minute.

"What were the physical features of this man?" James asked.

"He was short. Glasses seemed tight on the guy—"

"That sounds like Carl!" Tom exclaimed.

"Jared Moututou, you are under arrest for the murder of Carl Jubber on the night of the twelfth," James concluded, grabbing hold of Jared's arms.

"I just got out of that place!" Jared yelled. "I'm not going back in to serve a crime I didn't do!"

"We're not taking you to jail," Tom said.

"What?" James and Jared collectively said.

"Not until we know for sure you killed Carl Jubber. Until then, you'll be under house arrest at my place. My wife will take care of you."

Jared agreed to this deal and they all got in the car, where they headed back to Corner Cove to find out what exactly went down the night Carl Jubber died.

IV

Back at Tom's place, James, Tom, Anna, and Janis sit around the dinner table, staring at Jared. Jared felt awkward and didn't know what to say or when to say something. "So you do know who's responsible for this?" James said, breaking the silence.

"No! I don't even know the guy! I just bumped into him that night. Nothing else happened until *he* showed up," Jared confessed.

"He? Who's he?" Tom asked.

"About two years ago, the time the gunsluggers decided to disband, I was in the middle of a secret study in Area Fifty-One: the study of an alien species known as the Zardons. We were trying to figure out whether or not we should be threatened by this thing, but it got ahold of me and is now telling me what to do," Jared explained. "I don't know what to do anymore!"

"Can we speak to this Zardon?" Tom asked. Jared twitched for a second then fell silent; he awoke with an evil glare.

"What do you pathetic humans want?" the Zardon-Jared said.

James starts laughing. "What is this? Jared's clearly poking fun at science fiction here! Aliens aren't real!" Jared just stares at James and James stops laughing. "Wait, you're serious?"

"Jared, or ... Zardon ... why are you here?" Tom asked. Anna and Janis just sit there, listening to the entire scene, thinking of the ridiculous situations happening in their home.

"My master has sent me to get rid of you pathetic humans," Zardon-Jared replied. "And yes, I did kill the one you call 'Carl Jubber!'" This was when Janis stood up and ran to the other room in tears. Anna followed and the boys continued questioning the Zardon. Jared stares back at James and tells him, "Your record isn't as clean as people may think, if I recall, Eyebrows."

"Eyebrows?" Tom asked.

"Long story," James said, then punched the table in front of him. "You have no right to call me that!"

novel writing

"Why not? I am a member of the gunsluggers, am I not?" Jared pointed out.

"No, Jared is. You're not! You're just an imposter!" Tom shouted.

"Agent Pumpkin," Zardon-Jared said. "Nice to see you stoop down to the P.I. role."

"Get out of Jerry!" Tom shouted.

"My name isn't Jerry!" Zardon-Jared shouted as he pulled out the metal arm with the gun.

"Where did you get that?" James asked.

"I grabbed it on my way out of prison," Zardon-Jared explained. At that, James lunged forward and grabbed the gun. The arm fell clean off and the Zardon squealed, ooze dripping from the chair and onto the carpet next to James. Jared was back to himself. "Wh ... what happened?" Jared asked.

"Jared, you're going to be fine," James assured him. "Tom and I will find a cure for your problem."

"Cure? I don't remember a cure for alien symbiotism," Tom said.

"I know a place," James told him. Tom blindly followed, although he had no idea what was to come. He followed James into his office, where James used the arm to blast a portal in the sky.

"How did you do that?" Tom asked.

"I invented this thing," James said. "I left it in the vault, yet I never thought I'd get to see it again."

They both jump in and land in Area Fifty-One, where the original hideout of the gunsluggers once stood. "What are we doing in the middle of Area Fifty-One?" Tom asked.

James ignored him and knocked on the door to the building as he cried out the secret password, "Sandwich!" The door indeed opened and the two walked in being greeted by three agents from the gunslugger's rivals: the Today's Institute for Massive Explanation. T.I.M.E., for short.

novel writing

"What are you gunsluggers doing?" one agent asked. "This is our turf now!"

"Susan?" Tom said, revealing himself.

"Thomas?" the agent said back. She rushed towards him and they hugged one another. "What are you doing here? You should be in Corner Cove solving crimes!"

"That's what I'm doing," Tom said. "Solved a murder. Now I'm solving more of an identity theft case. What are you doing here, sis?"

"Since I'm a part of T.I.M.E., I'm here, working on saving the world from alien inhibitors," Susan said.

"That's what the gunsluggers were doing!" James shouted.

"Right," said the short one. "But no one asked them to steal a telescope too!"

James fell speechless and remained this way for a while.

novel writing

"What have you found out about a species called Zardon?" Tom asked, coming into full detective mode.

"Zardon bad," the brute said, lifting a container of toxic acid from one place to the high shelf.

"Who's the brute?" James asked.

"That's Mint," the short agent said. "He's been a dumb little guy since the gunsluggers accidentally poured the slimejuice on his head."

"Slimejuice? What slimejuice?" James asked.

"Rubberlink slime from the Invasion of Jellyzburg," the short one said. "It was the only time any aliens actually *invaded* our planet."

"So," Tom said, "is there a cure yet for symbiotism?"

Susan stared at her little brother, walked to a desk, and got out a container. "This is the only antidote for the symbiotism derived from the Zardons," she told him. "Don't mess this up!"

Crow-black Hair

Ellen Pan

Grade 9. East High School, Lincoln, NE. Francesca Rohrs, Educator. *Gold Key. American Voices Nominee.*

There is no country that serves me as a home.

I am no outcast if belonging to a country meant that I bore its people's features or that I owned a recognized passport of its kind, which are both criteria that I meet. But those factors made me a citizen and a stranger to everything else. For most of my life, I carried one question upon my back: where do I belong?

Let me start from the beginning of the story.

I was born a wailing baby in Pennsylvania, but not just any baby. I was a baby of Chinese descent—or as the traditional myths of China put it, a baby with dragon blood coursing through her veins.

Such a descendant of the dragons ought to have been born in China, shared her first breath of air with the red, flying five-starred flag that was the cloak of her motherland. But no, my first shrieking wail as I descended into the world boldly shattered all those rules. The name I took was a jumble of letters taken out of the *English* alphabet, and the passport that marked my existence was *blue* rather than red. With my sharp black hair, olive skin, and flat features, I stood out among the other fair-skinned newborns like—well, like a crane in a swarm of chickens, if you'd like to use the ancient Chinese proverb.

Of course I knew none of this back then. When I boarded my first-ever plane back to China, I was still a coughing baby—the kind that would wail during trips and annoy other passengers—and countries meant nothing more to me than pieces of dirt separated by imaginary lines.

After I started school in China, however, some things became a lot more evident. Because of my blue passport, my paperwork was noticeably more complicated than other children, and I had to be dragged along with my parents to confirm over and over again that yes, I was a registered human and no, I was *not* Chinese. Mountains of papers had to be signed in order for me to enroll in any school; more than once I saw a flinch in the teacher's face when my parents told them that this odd new student before them was *American*. I knew that something about me was *special* and it seemed not in a good way.

What did a six-year-old girl have to know about all this tiring business? But for those reasons I felt like a guest in the country that was supposed to be mine, the same land of dragons as the blood that coursed through my veins. I remember all the times I had cut into a strange class with strange faces in the middle of a school year, with forty pairs of brown eyes like mine trained upon me while the teacher did my introduction.

"All right, class. We have a new girl here today ... and she's *American.*"

It was as if my nationality was a thing to be ashamed of. I knew that slight blink of an eye, the sudden raise of a brow or the bare part of the lips, that signature tell everyone had when I told them that I wasn't born, by traditions, on Chinese grounds. From then on, they would look at me in a different way, whisper about the strange *American* girl in the halls. It seemed that nothing but my passport quarantined me from everyone else, because I bore the same signature crow-black hair and Asian features as any other child in my class. For a good chunk of my childhood, my biggest wish was to have a *red* passport like everyone else. That way I would fit in as a daughter of the dragons like I was born to be. How I envied those red booklets that signified the unity of a country! But my wish never came true, and the only mark of identification that I owned was the blue booklet that had followed me and weighed me down since my first shrieking cry in that hospital in Pennsylvania sealed my fate as an American.

It was a while before my classmates exposed their interest in my unique identity, but the questions eventually came.

"What's your name?" a girl who sat next to me in class asked me one day, halfway through her book.

I looked at her quizzically; we had been in the same class for months. I told her my Chinese name, the one that I had always assumed to be inferior to my English one.

personal essay & memoir

The girl shook her head, her glossy braids flinging from side to side. "No, the *other* one. Your English name."

I told her reluctantly. It was strange hearing the word—how the tone was so different, *foreign* from the leaping pronunciation of Chinese.

The girl furrowed her brows. "That sounds fancy," she finally decided. "So were you born in America?"

"Yeah."

Two pairs of brown eyes stared into each other.

"So you're not a real descendant of the dragons."

"What do you mean? I live here. My parents are Chinese, I speak Chinese—"

"But you have an English name, an American passport, and you were *born* in America. That makes you a fake Chinese, no matter how much you look like one," she said matter-of-factly. I had no better reply, so I watched as she swung her glossy braids behind her shoulders and continued reading on.

The girl's words grew more layers of meaning as I grew older, but back then, when I was six years old, they hit me with less shock or anger than confusion. How could I, having been in China for years, breathing its air and walking its surface every day of my life, be a *fake* Chinese? If I wasn't a true daughter of the dragons, I didn't know who was. I realized then that to the eyes of someone who had been born and raised on Chinese earth the *right* way, an idea as simple as someone with dragon blood taking a name built out of English letters was an act of betrayal on its own.

And so I sang the national anthem every Monday morning with feeble, unreal pride in my voice, watched the red five-starred flag rise in the wind. All the while I was fearing that the bright flag of the dragons had turned its back on me, a traitor from the West. I thought for a long time that my stark blue passport was what made me a drop of oil floating on water, preventing me from blending in although my physical features suggested like nothing else that I was truly a daughter of the dragons. But if I weren't Chinese, I wasn't sure that a blue passport and my birth in a Pennsylvanian hospital made me any more American.

That suspicion was proved when I was brought to Virginia for school, weaponless save for the flying papers that told everyone I was born in this country. I spoke little English, if the small portion of the language that I knew was intelligible to others at all when exiting my lips, burdened with the heavy, chipped accent of a stranger to this land. Not only had the language barrier set me apart from others but my physical features had betrayed me as well. No more worries for a blue passport wedged between reds—my black hair said it all. It was a soot stain among a sea of bobbing blondes and brunettes. Countless times I had inspected the mesmerizing way the other girls' hair flowed—shimmering fines strands like spun gold, twisting into lovely curls soft as clouds in the sky. My hair was a dull black, devoid of vibrance and jagged as a crow's stiff feathers. It never submitted to any type of curlers or pins, and strands would always spring out in the most awkward places when my hair was put up in any style more complicated than a ponytail. I was a crow, perched between countless birds of other feathers.

As much as I consciously tried to subdue the hair with hats and hoods, kept my head down to shield my face from view, I was still constantly pestered with questions. If I was a true American, why didn't I speak English? Why did I sit for two months at the nuts free table with peanut butter, thinking that free nuts would come my way? If I was a true American, why couldn't I even sing the anthem or have the pledge of allegiance ready on the tip of my tongue each morning? I had no answers to any of those questions.

For years my crossed identity bothered me nonstop. It felt at times that neither countries were willing to accept my existence, because I was an oddity that broke their traditional rules. I kept my head low whenever I was asked about my appearance or nationality; I dreamed of being a *right* Chinese or American, one that followed the traditional ways like everyone else I saw at school. Perhaps then I wouldn't be judged for all the sharp angles that I had, and I would be able to fit into a home country at last. Strange as it seemed, however, I was not growing to fit in anywhere. I learned to speak flawless English and Chinese yet spoke them with caution; I never mentioned a single word of being a daughter of the dragons or being born under the flying star-spangled banner.

At one point, I realized that it was not what others thought of me but what *I* thought of me that made all the difference. Simply because I was born on one piece of land rather than another didn't make any difference to where I belonged; it was me who cowered to stereotypes, prejudices, and eventually turned down the gates to both of my homes. Is there a reason for me to hide my crow-black hair under hats and hoods when I walk among people that don't share my features? A crow's feathers are nothing to be ashamed of.

Another August, another beginning of a school year. I flew all the way from China to Nebraska, filled in all of my too many forms for attending school, and when I stood at the front of the room, forty pairs of eyes trained on me, I told them that I was a daughter of the dragons without waver in my voice. I told them about my relentless, tumbling journeys between America and China each year, about my dual identity, about the red and gold of dragons in my heart and the star-spangled banner upon my back. In telling them all of this, I felt not the slightest bit of shame.

I had once longed to shed my black hair like crows shed feathers, hoped to fit in, be unnoticeable and plain, but that wish never came true. Now I wear my jagged, stark black locks like a glorious crown and let go by the eyes that looked my way. What did hair color matter? I wouldn't have minded if it were blonde or brunette or any other color in the world. It didn't matter to be Chinese or American by the proof of genes or documents, I learned, but by real pride in their culture. A crow's feathers or a robin's feathers be it, there was no difference. With each passing year, I molted my feathers like a crow in winter and sprouted new ones in the spring.

The feathers remained black like always, but the crow was a different one that could fly.

Tell me what makes me belong to one country or another. Legal forms? I have both red and blue in my hands. Languages? I speak both Chinese and English with ease; I harness the ability to throw behind the crutches of chewed-up translations. Through the ups and downs of growing up, between hurried flights from one side of the world to another, I saw past the twining stereotypes to the root of what finally settled my homeland. It's not the symbols printed on my passport, the earth that I walk upon, or the colors of my skin, hair, and eyes that make the choice; it's what I choose to be rather than what I let myself be shaped into through the eyes of others, and that decision alone solely defines the place I belong.

What is my nationality, you might ask? Well, you see, my country is one like no other. It stretches across the world, from eastern Asia across the Pacific Ocean to North America. I am both Chinese and American; I need no passport nor appearance to prove me right, for the choice I make, the will within me—that's the strongest power I hold.

The Things I Inherited from My Father

Tess Bowler

Grade 11. Duchesne Academy, Omaha, NE. Thomas Becker, Educator. *Silver Key.*

personal essay & memoir

Growing up, people used to tell me I looked like my mother. Despite this being the case, I couldn't help but refute it. At that age, I was going through a phase where I thought my mom was the worst and my dad was the best. See, my parents divorced when I was seven and everything seemed so black and white. I loved my dad and wanted to emulate him because he was the fun guy—showing me scary movies, staying up late, and introducing me to art. On the other hand, my adolescent brain, with little grasp of hard decisions, resented my mom. I felt hurt because my life was uprooted from Chicago to Omaha, because she worked all the time, because she was always keeping me on the straight and narrow. So when people told me I looked like my mom, I took that as an insult, that I was the opposite of my father because that's all my mom was to me.

As time went on, my rose-colored goggles began to fade. I started to see my father for the imperfect man he was—inconsistent and forgetful, never on time, and distant. My view of my mother also changed. She was not as disagreeable as my younger self remembered and she was strong, always working tirelessly to guarantee that I had a good life. The more I grew up, the more I realized that I did look like my mother, inheriting everything but her bleach blonde hair. My feelings about my parents were always mercurial, but it wasn't until my later teenage years that I learned things that would affect me forever, things regarding my parents' divorce. This knowledge came not as a consolidated discussion, but as small mentions, much like the problems in my parents' marriage that amassed over time. I once remarked to my mother about how my father would sometimes be gone for hours without telling me where he was and she only responded with, "That isn't anything new." When talking over lunch, we discussed how he was outwardly nice—always holding the door for people or offering to do chores—but he never came through on the things that counted. My mother was disappointed but not surprised that I had witnessed this behavior firsthand, as she had many years ago.

These discussions resulted in the turning of the tide to resentment towards my father instead of my mother. This distaste, combined with my mother dropping subtle hints that the disintegration of their marriage was caused by my father's infidelity, sent me over the edge. My mother was the best and my dad was the worst.

In the mirror, I now saw not my father's green eyes, but my mother's lips. The dark hair that framed my face was no match for the beautiful smile that I could only attribute to my mother. As much as I embraced my mother's physical features and disregarded my father's, an incident soon made me realize that the things you inherit from your parents are not always visible.

It was a warm night in September and school had just begun. After a party, I was given the job to drive two of my friends home (who were more or less inebriated). One of them was actually more of a friend of a friend, but the other was a boy I've known for years. See, it's complicated. I grew up, in my more formative years, with his twin sister as my best friend. I watched his baseball games, saw him every time I went over to her house, and spent countless family dinners sitting across from him. But it wasn't until that summer that I realized I was infatuated with him. I smiled, he smiled back. I made a joke, he laughed. He stole my phone, I chased him. He complained about his longtime girlfriend, I listened. So, that night when I dropped him off, he kissed me and I kissed back. As bad as it sounds, I didn't think about what I was doing. I didn't think about his girlfriend. I only thought about him. I wonder now if this is how the woman who my dad cheated on my mom with felt.

When I dropped him off, my phone was on silent, quieting the impending calls of my mother. I failed to realize until I was greeted by my sobbing mother on the end of the line that I was supposed it be home 45 minutes ago. It was 12:45 AM. After speeding home and attempting to construct a lie about where I had been and what I had been doing, my mom responded in a cold tone, "You're just like your father. Staying out, doing God knows what and not telling me where you are." With that, she disappeared upstairs, and I was left with the realization that maybe I was more like my father than I thought. No, I didn't have his nose, but I had his habit of absence without a warning of where I was. It was not his eyes I had inherited but the superficial quality of his actions. When people tell me I'm one of the nicest people they've ever met, I act humbly, not because I'm flattered, but because I don't think genuinely nice people disregard others' feelings so quickly like I had. Sure, I did not get the quality of infidelity from my dad, but I was no better than the woman who ruined my parents' marriage. Physically, I may not resemble my father, but when I look in the mirror I see more similarities than I would like to.

It Was an Accident

Daisy Friedman

Grade 11. Central High School, Omaha, NE. Hillary Blayney, Educator. *Silver Key.*

personal essay & memoir

It's okay, you're okay, just breathe. It was just an accident. Get your hands to stop shaking. He's in the next room, he's sitting on the bed, and he feels terrible. Stop it, calm down, you're fine. It was just an accident. "Should I rinse my mouth out?" You probably should because it tastes disgusting, but this is your first time, ha ha. It should be something you want to remember. You're *supposed* to like it. You liked it. It's fine, You're fine. Just get your act together and open the door. Okay, cool, walk into the room. Look at him, but not in the eyes. If you look at him in the eyes, you'll start shaking. Why is he sitting on the edge of the bed? Why is his head in his hands? He looks like he's actually about to cry. You should really be going over there and comforting him. He knows he messed up, so it's fine. Besides, you should've been clearer about what you wanted. Do not make it obvious you're uncomfortable. You shouldn't even be uncomfortable. He's a good person, he's your person, he wouldn't hurt you. That's right, sit on the bed and give him a little kiss on the cheek ... there we g—That felt so different. What's the word? Menacing. It felt menacing. Why isn't he looking at you? "Please, look at me. Look at me or ... or ... kiss me. Tell me it was just an accident!"

He looked up and said he was sorry, that he was an idiot. Sorry? Sorry for what? He didn't do anything wrong, he couldn't have. You can hear your heartbeat in your ears. Please just push it (the heartbeat) out. If he's apologizing, that means he feels bad for something, which means he's done something wrong. That means it's his fault, but of course it's not his fault. You let it happen. You didn't try hard enough to stop it. Did you even motion to him? He's not a mind reader, he didn't see it. You didn't even move, why didn't you move? His hand wasn't even pushing down that hard. Clearly you wanted it, even though you said you were unsure, but you agreed anyway. You wanted what he wanted. He never asked you what you wanted. Why didn't he ask you what you wanted? That doesn't matter because you let him follow through with it. So now this is your mess to clean up. Go on, fix it. Yeah, there you go, touch his face super gently and run your fingers through his hair.

Why is there such a weird silence? He's clearly thinking something. You can see the wheels in his head turning. He says that his body just froze. You just stopped breathing. Your breathing is getting really rapid and you very well might pass out. Your hands are shaking. What does that mean? How can he just freeze? He's a fifteen-year-old, and he has control of his body. Oh, my god. There is blood rushing to your cheeks. Stop being mad. This is all a big misunderstanding, just calm down. Say that it's okay. Say you know he didn't mean to do it. It's so much easier to avoid the conflict. He hates this "feminism bullshit." Just keep saying it. "It's okay." But it's not okay. "You're okay." Get out of my house. "You're safe." You are not safe. "It's not a big deal." It is a big deal. Tell him to get out of your room, get off your bed, take his coat, and go. Why are you not saying any of this out loud? There is nothing stopping me from kicking him out right now. Yes, but also what would he tell his mom? Okay fine, if you can't say that, you need to stop apologizing. What kind of a feminist are you? What kind of a woman are you? "I want my mom." He starts to perk up. He says he's okay if I'm okay. "Yes, I'm okay." No, you are not okay. No, you don't want his hand there. No, don't let him touch your leg like that. Stop letting him touch you, please stop! Okay, fine, one kiss. It'll return things to normalcy, right? Okay, his mom just pulled into the driveway. Yeah, sure, walk out like it's any old day. "Okay, bye, love you." Silence. Go back to the bedroom. The sheets smell like him. "I want to go home," but you are home. No, you are in your house, this is your bed, but this room ... this is not your home anymore and this was not an accident.

Over the Fire

Ellen Pan

Grade 9. East High School, Lincoln, NE. Francesca Rohrs, Educator. *Honorable Mention.*

"Come on, jump over the fire and Dad will be free."

My eyes flew open in the dark. The tingling dream on the edge of my mind faded away almost instantly as my body pulled itself from sleep. A thirst lingered in my throat.

It was nearly a routine for me. At some point in the night, my eyes would open to an expanse of inky darkness that was no different from the back of my eyelids.

Through the slumbering house I stole, the air around me so dense that seeing eyes might as well have been blind. Still I kept them wide open as I drew up an imagination of where everything was—the door to my left, the hallway quiet and deserted.

My feet found the eight stairs that connected the second floor to the first; they stepped across the line that marked the end of carpet and the start of cool wooden planks.

I made my way to the kitchen counter and quenched the strangling thirst at my throat like I did every night.

personal essay & memoir

But, before I started back upstairs, I stood and stared into the darkness for a long time.

My imagination slowly created a hunched shape of Dad sitting at the couch, tapping his foot while reading *A Brief History of Nearly Everything*. I imagined his index finger trailing across the line that he was reading, his expressions wrinkled by a concentrated frown.

Maybe he's really there, I thought, despite the absurdness of my hopes. *Maybe Dad came back.*

But I knew that it wasn't possible for I had leapt over the fire, and the fire's decision was definite.

Still I reached out to the wall and flipped on the lights. Color pierced through the film of darkness; there was nothing on the couch.

I turned the lights off and went back to sleep.

....

It's hard to believe that one month ago Dad had been here to visit me in this very house. We exchanged stories; he told me about his new interest in cycling, and I told him about school.

"I could have done better on the test," I sighed as Dad flipped through my textbook. "There was so much more potential."

He only shrugged. "Doesn't matter."

"What if I got a zero?"

Another shrug, a smile this time. "Doesn't matter."

"What about the time I got first place?"

"That's awesome, but it still doesn't matter."

I threw up my hands in mock frustration, though I couldn't suppress the grin tugging at the corner of my mouth. "Doesn't matter, doesn't matter. Nothing matters to you, does it?"

Dad shut the textbook and tossed it aside, where it joined the spew of other miscellaneous things laid across my bedroom floor.

"What does matter is the future. If you didn't do well on a test, make it better next time. If you did do well, keep it up. If your house burned down, make more money and buy another one. What's the point of dwelling on the past? Enjoy your now and your future, that's what's important."

I sighed and shook my head. "Is everything in the past just *gone* to you?"

He winked. "I have memories, of course. But, as beautiful and tantalizing as memories might be, they dwell in the past. Only the future holds weight."

Dad leaned against my chair and picked up another book that was lying sprawled on my floor. *A Brief History of Nearly Everything*, it read.

It was the last night of Dad's stay in Nebraska. The next morning he would be on a plane flying back to China. At the time I didn't know why, but a strange, uneasy feeling dawned upon me.

I didn't believe in prophecies, but this one came true. Just two weeks later I boarded a plane to China, following Dad's steps. By then everything had already been set in stone, shrouded in black.

....

I will not talk about what Dad's body looked like, nor what air hung in the room at the formal funeral. Those words are meant for another story. All I will say is that I watched in stiff shock as Dad's coffin entered the cremator in a shower of sparks, all forty-nine years of knowledge, memories, hopes, and plans reduced to ash and nothing more.

"He's grown tired, of course," Aunt told me after the formal funeral was over, both her wrinkled hands holding mine. "Forty-nine years! You haven't lived nearly half that long. He's so stressed out after this long. Death is a relief to him, I think. Now he's in the Underworld beneath our feet, joined with your Grandma."

Aunt held me like this for a long time, all the myths about death and the afterlife that she had ever known of pouring out from between her lips. She told me about Yan, the god of death; about ghosts hiding in the night; about the world of the dead, where there was no more suffering for those who had earned their rest by cutting through the rough life that they lived above ground.

"I know he didn't mean to leave you like this, but what's already happened can't be reversed." Aunt tucked a lock of loose hair behind my ear. "No one knows my brother better than I do ... I know he wouldn't want you to waste your young cheeks away with tears. Keep all the memories here"—she put her fingers to my temples. "As long as you believe he's there, he will stay with you. But remember, as beautiful and tantalizing as the memories might be, they dwell in the past. Only the future holds weight."

The traditional funeral was the part that I really cared about. It took place in the tiny town that Dad grew up in with the name of Huang-gang. It was a place where old grandmothers and young children were not yet too burdened down by the thought of work to forget about myths and magic. Dad's real funeral deserved to be hosted in his hometown.

The ceremony lasted days, each one smoldering with the scent of lit incense. Aunt lit handfuls of them at a time, planting them in golden pots to shrivel away while she kneeled in front of them, reading from her ancient book of spells to keep Dad's spirit safe on his descent to the Underworld. The monotone of speech would sometimes last for hours, lulling everything near it into a mythical trance.

The funeral wasn't a dank, gray gathering in a tall room like the previous one. If possible, the house grew more lively, with countless relatives and friends streaming in through the door every minute, some of whom I had never even seen the faces of. They threw flowers to the ceiling and sang their goodbyes, cooked grand meals that were set before Dad's framed picture so that his spirit could enjoy a last meal before entering the world of the dead. Aunt's endless monotone of chanting continued on for the entire day and well into the night before she decided that Dad was finally safe enough.

....

On the third day since Dad's soul left his body, Aunt cut my hair.

I sat in a chair too small for me, neck uncomfortably scratchy with the plastic sheet tied around it. I had suggested going to the nearby barber to get a haircut, but Aunt would hear none of it. "How will I know if he gets the hair if I don't do it myself?" she demanded.

The room was quiet save for Aunt's unintelligible chanting and the constant snipping of scissors swimming through my hair. With each snip my head felt lighter, relieved from another lock of burden. By the end of the haircut, a thick mattress had formed on the floor behind my chair.

Aunt ceased her chanting at last and told me that I could finally be set free from the plastic sheet. I watched as she carefully swept up every strand of the fallen hair into a dustpan and poured it all into the glowing orange fireplace, where it was immediately disintegrated in a puff of ill-smelling fumes.

"The traditions have to be followed, dear." Aunt exhaled as she stood up, all the hair burnt. "The legends in Huang-gang say that when a mother or father enters the Underworld, Yan first casts them in a dark ravine. The only way to escape is by using their children's hair as a braided rope, which they can receive through fire and use climb up to heaven."

I didn't question her story. Anything past the border of life was unknown to me, so why wouldn't her tales be the truth? All I could hope for right then, with the stinging scent of burnt keratin in my nose, was that my hair was long enough to reach from the top of the ravine to the bottom and that the braided rope was strong enough for Dad to climb to heaven where he would be safe with Grandma at last.

....

On the seventh day, it was by Huang-gang traditions to go to the graveyard. There, Dad's ashes would be set under the earth and sealed away forever. The crew today was more scattered with only the closest family members aboard.

"When we're passing under a bridge or through a tunnel, tell Dad to follow along. Ghosts don't know how to navigate through these spaces, but your dad will be able to recognize his beloved daughter's voice and he will be able to follow us to the graveyard, where he will finally make his descent into the world that we can't enter." Aunt urged me as she was flinging stacks of yellow paper outside the car window.

"Dad, hurry up and follow me, come to the graveyard where you'll be free. Though through this darkness you cannot see, follow my voice and the words I speak."

That was the spell Aunt taught me. Spoken in Chinese, it had a strangely eerie effect. The rolling of each word off of my tongue, I imagined, was a thin, bright line drawn in the darkness for Dad's spirit to follow. I sang the rhyme every time the world was dimmed by the shadow of a bridge or tunnel until my mouth had run dry.

It was a long, tedious drive up to the mountains where the local graveyard was located.

"Hold Dad's photo in front of you all the time," my aunt ranted on as we ascended the circles of winding roads. "That's right, hold it just like this so that Dad can see, be able to find his way home—don't turn it around."

I held the framed photo up in front of me as I watched from the rearview mirror. Litters of yellow paper flew out of the car's back window, fluttering in the wind like fallen leaves.

"What's the paper for?" I asked.

"It's the currency of the Underworld, dear. The roads we're taking now are the property of the mighty Yan, and he wouldn't let Dad's spirit come with us unless we pay him good money for it."

The yellow paper kissed the road and disappeared from sight when we rounded the corner.

....

The car came to a screeching halt at the entrance of the graveyard, half-sunken in a swamp of gray mud. The rest of the trip, it seemed, we would have to deal with on our own.

I exited the car first, holding Dad's framed picture in front of me while the rest of the crew poured out from the car. We walked in a stiff line until I reached the gravestone that bore no name, stark white amidst the crowd. Grandma's gravestone had her name engraved in shining gold, in memory of her glorious long life; Aunt said that Dad's name wouldn't be added until three years later because his age of death was too young for display.

Three years. I'd be eighteen by then, a full-grown woman with my own life ahead of me. The idea was scary.

I watched from a distance as the workers lowered the urn into the tiny stone chamber beneath the earth. The shadows of the alive, Aunt said, should not be sealed into the grave with the dead. It was at that moment that I realized the sheer distance that now stood like a brick wall between Dad and me. We had parted ways and lived in different worlds. With a sharp clap, the two slabs of concrete on top sealed all daylight from the grave, bonded together with hot glue. The sound was final, condescending, and it split my heart.

I knew that the preparation for Dad's journey was at an end when the ritual of money-burning came. A sack lay on the ground, bright yellow rolls of paper tumbling out of its gaping mouth. The paper shared many similarities with the money that was used to pay Yan for passage on the roads, but this was more detailed, carefully manufactured with fine illustrations of mythical Chinese beasts engraved within the paper. *Ten thousand* was written in delicate calligraphy on each sheet, rolls upon rolls of it. I wondered about the inflation rates in the Underworld but decided that Dad would be fine.

We burned the money under the glaring gray eye of the sky, watching as golden flames ate up cash like a starved monster, twisting them into tiny bits of black ash and sending them to the Underworld. The fire was like a million dancing fairies hand in hand, singing unheard songs.

Fire had a lot to do with Huang-gang customs; it was the messenger of souls, the link between two opposite worlds. Incense was lit with fire, notes were sent with the strike of a match, and anything else that needed to make its way to the Underworld was piled up in a tall heap, then reduced to ashes and nothing more.

We burned the whole sack of Underworld money, little by little, until all that remained of the yellow paper was a soft circle of soot. The winds flew by and drank up all the blue smoke, carrying it far, far away.

"Well, everything's set now," Aunt said shakily, and for the first time in days I saw tears well up in her eyes.

The few of us made our way down the mossy stone steps, past what must have been thousands of gravestones. Some were weathered, their golden engravings long blackened with age; some were ivory white, brand new like Dad's was. I couldn't help but wonder if their owners' souls were safe in the Underworld now or if they were still drifting about in agony, waiting for the first seven days of their death to be over.

We halted at the exit of the cemetery, where green trees and paved paths awaited before us. The last ritual was a pile of burning branches blocking the gate, its low flames splayed out and licking the ground.

It was there that the final part of the ceremony came, the last touch to the preparation for Dad's journey. Though I knew that this was inevitable, my heart was still reluctant as if weighed down by a thousand deceased souls.

"Jump over the fire," Aunt told me. Everyone else had already done so, standing on the other side of the gate, huddled in their jackets.

"Jump over the fire," she repeated, with a look of unease in her eyes. "You have your father's spirit clinging to your back. You were the dearest to him when he was alive, and so he couldn't shake away thoughts of you even as his soul fled from his white bones. Only those with warm blood rushing through their veins could pass over fire while ghosts are left behind. If you jump over it, Dad will be able to let go and be free in the Underworld at last."

I looked down at the fire. It was a strange flitting thing, its many tongues lashing out at the gray air. In my mind, I imagined Dad standing behind me. Strangely, I thought of the ancient Greek tale of Orpheus with the spirit of his wife following him, invisible and nonexistent in the dark. For a second, I almost believed that if I turned around, Dad would be behind me in the brown sweater that he wore the last time he came to visit me, *A Brief History of Nearly Everything* in his hands. He would smile at me like this was all a joke and pull me into his arms.

The fire was a million dancing figures beckoning at me. Golden sparks flew out of the top and drifted into the sky to become stars.

"Come on," my aunt told me. Her cheeks were growing red from the cold. "Jump over those branches and Dad will be free."

Memories, however beautiful and tantalizing as they might be, dwell in the past. Only the future holds weight.

I leapt over the fire and didn't look back once.

Dear Organ Donor

Daisy Friedman

Grade 11. Central High School, Omaha, NE. Hillary Blayney, Educator. *Gold Key. American Voices Nominee.*

poetry

Dear organ donor,
I know you will never know me, but the evening of July 20th, 2006, you saved my life.
We were only 3 years old.
I celebrated that day, my grandpa and I had a tea party in my basement and sang l'chaim "to life!"
Maybe that night while I was celebrating,
your family was holding your hand with tear-streaked faces and said,
"It's okay, baby, you can let go, we'll see you soon."
I'm sorry.
Dear organ donor,
In 2008 I started kindergarten,
and my mom put my hair in pigtails.
This doesn't seem like a big deal, but it was for me.
I was so happy it was growing back just long enough for them to hold.
Mine wasn't the typical kindergarten farewell.
I kissed my parents, and they had tears in their eyes.
But theirs were tears of joy.

tears that symbolized the bridge,
the bridge from abnormality to normalcy
from sickness to health.
I skipped along, lunchbox in hand and backpack on
back
filled not with books, but with a feeding tube.
And as they sent me on my way,
they thought of you.
Dear organ donor,
Not a moment goes by where I don't feel at least a little
bit guilty.
Guilty the moment your organs were put into my body
was the best moment of my life.
Guilty that on that same day you departed this planet
with less than what you came in with.
Guilty that I hate my scars.
Guilty that I want to feel beautiful.
Guilty that you will never be able to walk this earth,
feel the ground under your little feet.
Guilty that I'm breathing.
You were only 3 years old.
Dear organ donor,
When I was eight, I performed on stage for the first
time.
The lights beamed into my eyes.
The energy of the ensemble was euphoric.

poetry

Acting is simply embodying another person's existence.
For the first time in my life, I was able to escape from myself.
Dear organ donor,
People don't understand what it was like to be sick.
Sitting in a hospital bed, dreaming of tomorrow.
Fluids pumping into my body that were keeping me alive, while killing me slowly.
I didn't understand what was happening.
I've always been told that I am the bravest kid out there,
but what about you?
You gave me the miracle of life.
There are so many things my parents hid from me.
How do you tell a toddler they are dying?
I was only 3 years old.
Dear organ donor,
I find it hard to understand in my mind, what it means
to love someone you've never met.
I love you in so many ways,
but not romantically,
In a way I can only express to the person who saved my life.
A love and admiration so deep and so sincere, it is naturally only reserved for you.
Dear Organ Donor,

Today I wrote a letter to you.
I wanted to sooner, but I didn't know where to start.
You gave me a second chance at life.
I managed to walk away unscathed, with just a scar.
But you, you are dead.
And what do I say to your family?
I am the 15-year-old girl who received the precious gift
  from your child.
I know I will never be able to thank you enough for
  giving me a second chance at life.
I would also like to say how sorry I am for your loss.
Nothing would ever be enough.
Maybe I would say, I would give it all up to put your
  family all back together again.
But if given the opportunity, would I?
Dear Organ Donor,
January 30th was my Bat Mitzvah
the day of my life states I am no longer a child.
Everybody I loved was in a room to support me on a
  day nobody thought I'd live to see.
And I did, because of you.
It was a day where I am called to the Torah as an adult,
a daughter of a mitzvah.
I felt you there next to me, your hand on my shoulder
  as I chanted:
Y'hei sh'lama raba min sh'maya

May there be an abundance of peace for you in
Heaven.
Dear Organ Donor,
I want to make you proud.
I wanted you to know you died a hero, my hero.
The greatest hero I will never know
and I promise to take good care of you,
to honor you with everything I do.
Because, on the night of July 20th, 2006, you saved my
life.
Dear Organ Donor,
Thank you.

I Am the ABC

Jingming Yu

Grade 11. East High School, Lincoln, NE. Sarah Staples-Farmer, Educator. *Gold Key. American Voices Nominee.*

That I listed throughout the days of my unripe kindergarten times
The deviation of my mother's tongue and my father's absence,
A stranger to a land underneath me,
On a sphere following an endless circle.

School is a dangerous land,
Where Asia is China and China is a continent,
And China vaguely resembles a chicken,
And the parent of my parent lives on the tip of the wattle,
Where I visit them every summer after the last day of school
Where my mother adopts me into a motherland I wasn't born from.

After school, I don't invite my friends to my house,
Which is a kingdom foreign to their own,

poetry

Reeking of fresh, steamed rice and the family-recipe
fish,
A mixture of words that contain the sounds of chimes
followed by druid incantations.
My mother isn't good at magic.

I learn that I can't learn to multiply,
And why a negative and a negative is a positive.
When the couple comes back from the restaurant
I do not know why Tom kills Wendy,
Nor do I find out that Tom is a cat and Wendy is a fish.
I'm caught in a riddle asking too many questions too
far from the solution.
I'm supposed to be good at school.
I'm supposed to be know instruments.
I'm supposed to be smart.

I've known the alphabet since I was five.

The Redwoods, Melody of the Forest, Velcro, Pen and Ink

Olivia Achtemeier

Grade 9. Beatrice High School, Beatrice, NE. Jodi Fakler, Educator. *Silver Key.*

The Redwoods

They tower high, with nothing but the sound of
their leaves rustling against one another. Thousands
together, but yet surrounded by nothing but insects
and birds.

The banana slugs climb the towering trunks,
venture through the vines, get lost in the ferns.
The snails stick low to the ground, hoping to remain
hidden, not to be seen.

The steep ground, nature's slide. With fallen, hollow
trees, once home to birds, now home to rodents and
overcome to the old now growing the new.

The silence disturbed by the peaceful sound of water
rushing over, polishing rocks, only to be able to pass
with fallen trunks.

Every now and then things become still, nothing moves. The trees tower high. Thousands together, but yet surrounded by nothing but insects and birds.

Melody of the Forest

The creek sings its lullaby
The trees rustle their leaves
As moss climbs their trunks
The sun can barely be seen

The creek reaches its chorus
The sharp smells fill the forest
As fall approaches,
The trees hum along to the tune

The wind settles down
The leaves hush
As the world falls asleep,
The creek's soothing melody begins once again

Velcro

Gray and sleek
Large and tall
Four paws,
A stub for a tail

Laps water
Slobber and drool
Full of energy,
Runs orbits around the pool

Loud bark
Floppy ears
Runs at squirrels,
He listens and hears

Chews on his blanket
Makes shanks from toy bones
Curls up on the floor
And sleeps when at home

A lot like my shadow,
Lays at my feet
When I walk in the door
It's he who greets

Pen and Ink

Pencil brushes paper
Pen dips in ink
Lines form,
Words created

Paint covers canvas
Keyboard clicks on letters
Shapes form,
Paragraphs created

Colors fill in the lines
Papers complete by stanzas
Pictures form,
Stories created

Jazz Age Love

Daisy Friedman

Grade 11. Central High School, Omaha, NE. Hillary Blayney, Educator. *Silver Key.*

I want to be loved like the 1920s.
I want to be loved like flourishing flapper dresses,
gleaming, scarlet lips, and finger waves.
I want to be loved like moving picture magic
Hold me in your arms like I'm Louise Brooks,
Just like in silent films ...
We don't need words to form passion,
just you and me inside your Model T.
I want to be loved like the 1920s
I want to be loved like underground speakeasies.
Drink me in like I'm an Old Fashioned.
Like concealed flasks filled
to fuel the night's adventures.
We'll hide our desires under our tweed coats
just like the bootleggers.
I want to be loved like the 1920s.
I want to be the Daisy to your Gatsby.
Look at me with anxious eyes,
Fall deeper in love every minute.
Let me be your guiding green light.

poetry

I want to be loved like the 1920s.
I want to be loved like Jazz music.
Sing to me sweetly the words of Louis Armstrong,
Because in your arms I think to myself,
What a wonderful world.
Let life be an intoxicating dance party
As we foxtrot in time.
I want to be loved like the 1920s
I want to be loved like Wall Street
Make me an ignorant fool, teach me to forget
how to behave with our newfangled freedom.
And when it all comes crashing down,
We'll still have our memories.
I want to be loved like the 1920s
Preserve me in sepia tones, and
paint with the glaze of an archaic era,
In a silk Charleston negligee.
And I want to be loved like the 1920s
Never wanting to stop the party,
Never wanting to slow the pace.

VOLCANO

MALIK GILLESPIE

Grade 12. Westside High School, Omaha, NE. Dana Rose, Educator. *Silver Key.*

Portfolio Silver Key

I describe my sister as a force of nature.
She is all the colors of all the best sunsets,
The crash of the ocean's waves upon the beach,
The soft swells of snow in the winter and
The glitter of ice sheets
When the light hits it just right

On her Good Days,
She's vibrant
like the colors of a meadow in full bloom;
Flower blossoms sprout from her throat,
Roses without thorns replace words,
Skin and smiles like stolen starlight,
And bottled lightning in her eyes.
Her laugh makes me feel as if
There was never a reason to cry,
As if there were no cloudy days,
never a need for rain boots.

It took me years to learn what Borderline meant
"Personality Disorder"
Was a phrase with the meaning blown away
By my young lips struggling to say them,
And struggling more to understand them.
When my mother sat at the dining room table
And cried a waterfall's worth of tears while sitting in
    the aftermath,
I'd tell her it was okay. It was just that
The volcano in my sister's head had erupted.

The Bad Days are the days
That the rageful hot magma builds up
And lava flows from her lips.
My mother was always burned the worst,
But I still seemed to choke on the smoke.

On the Bad Days,
My sister is a new Vesuvius.
And my house a new Pompeii
How do people claim to understand
When I say I know how fallout clings to you
Long after you think you've washed it off;
How ash can still be found
In the corners of our kitchen
From dishes, thrown in anger, shattered
Like my early dreams of normality.

How can they claim to understand
The feeling of suffocation that comes with
Choking on your own voice,
And the guilt that comes later from not speaking up.

On the Bad Days,
She's a new Katrina
Leaving her own trail of debris,
Floods of broken glass
From our fallen family picture frames.
The warped wood of kitchen cabinets
And warped memories.
If I listen carefully, I swear
I can still hear how the walls contain
The echoes of her voice consumed the thunder.

As a child,
I didn't think it was abnormal
To know what my home looks like
After a storm slips in under the cracks of the door,
To be familiar with the sight
Of swirling storm clouds swallowing a family member.
To me, it was second nature
To feel the charge in the air
In the moments before lightning strikes, sudden,
Sparking a furious wildfire.
That taste of an angry storm brewing

Is as familiar on my tongue
As my sister's Sunday morning breakfasts.

I do not love the storm,
But I do love the shape they mold themselves into.
I love my sister, and every time I say it,
it will be louder than any roll of thunder and just as beautiful as she is.

Finding the Good in Something Terrible

Maryam Muayad

Grade 12. East High School, Lincoln, NE. Tina Le, Educator. *Silver Key.*

Walking through the garden of my memories
Waking up in the fear of everyone's eyes
only a couple of years old
I wanted to shout and say, "go away, this is our country" but I was unable to pronounce the words.
Instead, learning weapon names like AA-52, DS-32, L7A1, mortars
memorizing what they sounded like
making bets with friends on which one just went off
In our houses,
Hiding is all we did
Being silent is all we knew
Each other is all we had
Every time lights go off
Praying begins
Shooting gets closer
Screaming gets louder
And that ... was us

poetry

Peace is all we wanted but it was the only thing we couldn't have
We wanted to sleep for one day without having to wake up in fear
Wanted to stop alternating the watch at night and sleep all together
Even though we knew that couldn't happen
Walking through the garden of my memories
I know moving wasn't the best choice but we did not have a choice
We tried to forget the harsh memories but
Can we forget the terrible memories of war?
Can we forget the hunger we lived in?
The torture we lived through?
The sound of yelling that popped our eardrums?
The lies we told "mom I spilled water on myself by mistake"
when in reality it was us too afraid to go to the bathroom in the middle of the night?
The fear of strangers jumping in our tent pretending to be peaceful just so they can steal our stuff?
Or can I forget the scars from flying bomb fragments that marked my body inch by inch
And even if we did forget
Looking down at our scars will make us remember
Every time a lock down drill goes off at school, we'll remember.

Sometimes I wonder if my heart is going to stop
But it is still bleeding
Dark red blood
As red as a rose
Walking through the garden of my memories
Realizing that thistles were spreading I picked a rose
It was dark red and smelled astonishing
It poked my finger and caused it to bleed
Its beautiful red petals
with spikes poking everyone that touched it
it was half dead but still stood high with its green
    leaves pointing up
It reminded me that I am a survivor
I am still living
Hoping one day the world fills up with peace
as much as it is filled up with dark red beautiful roses
to remind us that we can find good things in some-
    thing terrible.

Disco

Alora Schneider

Grade 11. East High School, Lincoln, NE. Tina Le, Educator. *Silver Key.*

I don't know how to get myself out of this small town
I'd use the Great Gatsby as a metaphor for my obsession with moving to a coastal state, but I've never read the book
I think I need to finish high school before I decide where to go
But I think I want to go to that ancient beach with the dinosaur footprints
Because I enjoy permanence
Nothing is forever except saltine crumbs
In the carpet of the retirement home where I work
And me in this town, terrified of going to college
Maybe I could do what F. Scott Fitzgerald intended
Write a book about how to get to the American Dream
So I could pass go, collect 200 dollars
But my attention span is too short and I've never been great at spelling
Take me to the late '70s New York Disco Scene
Give me a neon time machine
I apologize for the chaos

I think like an out of tune piano
Disjointed and pointless
The point is I feel trapped in flyover state capitalism,
American Capitalism
Which I think we can all relate to
I am a disco ball, but the lights are off so I'll put on my
work shoes and feed the machine
And put out more saltine crackers
And never finish a poem
Because this is Nebraska and Disco has been dead for
years

Flying Free

Jenna Smith

Grade 8. Lefler Middle School, Lincoln, NE. Amy Sauer, Educator. *Silver Key.*

Dragons full of mighty power,
Anger of a tiger, sweet as a flower
Commanding the land, skies, and seas,
Earthquakes, volcanoes, and even a breeze
Beating wings and swinging tails,
Pointed spikes and shining scales

With claws that slash
And jaws that gnash
And eyes that pierce the darkness,
With flames burning bright
And a fiercely fought fight
And eyes that pierce the darkness,

With power for good
Or power for evil
One might never know,
So strong and still free
Their roars a melody
No one tells them where to go.

poetry

Fantasies of a small child
That never knew the word mild,
But while their fierce reputation
Spreads fear through the nation
The seed of imagination
Heeds only determination.

poetry

GRANDMA'S HOUSE

ELIZABETH GRANTHAM

Grade 12. Westside High School, Omaha, NE. Liz Hough, Educator. *Honorable Mention.*

It pains me to see you like this. To see your skin, once a vibrant shade of blue, now cracked and dry as paper.

To see your hair, once a deep, healthy green, now dark and greasy, with pieces of it missing from your scalp.

To see your once shiny eyes rendered completely useless, blinded from the uncountable boxes of clutter stacked up against them.

Yes, it hurts to see you like this.

poetry

But I remember when it didn't hurt.

I remember when coming to you was a gift, instead of a curse, when seeing your familiar body made me happy, instead of sad, when the joy you brought into my heart was pure instead of bittersweet.

Oh, yes, I remember.

Standing in front of you now, gazing into your broken eyes, all the memories flood back to me in a waterfall of painful images of happy things.

Gingerbread cookies, dressed in red icing and candy shoes, smiling nervously as a bunch of hungry kids rush into the kitchen to devour them.

A fire lighting up the living room, burning before a bunch of tired adults, who cheerfully talk amongst themselves, while enjoying a type of beverage I wasn't allowed to drink.

Chubby, toddler hands eagerly tearing at a box wrapped in colorful paper to reveal an even more colorful surprise.

Things were so much *simpler* back then. So much happier.

I wish I could go back. I wish *we* could go back.

But I can't and you can't and all we have left is a picture of who we were.

My friends tell me it's weird that I obsess over that picture so much, that I obsess over *you* so much, but they don't understand what you once were and how far you've fallen. They don't know that your counters were once filled with sugar and sprinkles and icing instead of old car magazines and cigarette butts and beer bottles.

They don't know that once you gathered a family together, pulling them from the corners of the world like a magnet, instead of a bunch of renters, from anywhere and everywhere, not caring who they were so long as they had money.

No, they don't know, and they don't care.

They see you as you are: a grief-stricken bachelor's house who fills you up with as many people as he can, so he won't feel so alone.

Once you didn't need to be filled up.

Once people would come without paying money or without looking you up online, they would just come because you were their home.

And they loved you.

We loved you.

But not anymore.

You hurt and break us as if you were our worst enemy instead of our childhood home.

You fill your insides with strangers and paint your walls so we won't recognize you, but we do.

And we receive your message loud and clear: we are not welcome.

Fine.

You're just a house anyway. No longer alive, already dead, slowly decaying each day that passes.

Obsessing over you isn't going to bring her back and loving you isn't going to make her breathe again.

You're just a house.

Just a worthless pile of bricks and wood, reeking of cigarette smoke and another woman's perfume.

You're nothing.

So, I'm done with you. I'm walking away and not looking back and I never want to see you again.

You've hurt me far too much for that. All you are is just a painful reminder of everything I had and just how much I lost. You're not Grandma's house anymore.

You're the renter's house.

You're the girlfriend's house.

You're the house I hate because you aren't the home I loved. You're just a house.

Just a worthless, stupid house that I foolishly talk to as if it's alive.

Goodbye, house! I'm moving on with my life and leaving you behind to rot.

With any luck the government will come and condemn you so I won't be tempted to wish such any ugly building would go back to the way it was.

You might as well be a pile of rubble already!

I don't care about you anymore or who you welcome inside.

By all means, shelter the college dropouts and the drug addicts and the people searching for a job!

By all means, take care of the pretty blonde woman who is far too young to be a wife, yet clings to my grandfather's arm anyway!

Do it! See what I care! Because I can already tell you that I care absolutely nothing!

Absolutely nothing at all.

I Can't Stay, but I Can't Leave

Kylie Ketelsen

Grade 12. Westside High School, Omaha, NE. Christina Nelson, Educator. *Honorable Mention.*

I can't go to sleep
Because what if I wake up and you're not here anymore
Or you're in a hospital bed with tubes in your arms
    and pills in your stomach
It's happened too many times before

Don't think I'll ever look at a bottle of Tylenol the
    same way
Not after the things I watched you do
The ambulance I had to make you call
Sitting on the other end of a FaceTime call
Hoping
Praying
I'm not even religious

When I was around you'd touch me
But the second I left you'd be back to touching a knife
Lighting up a cigarette 'cause you feel you can't go
    soon enough

poetry

Eating yourself away on the inside
Cutting yourself apart on the outside
While I stood and watched

And I know I tried to help you
I tried, but I just couldn't be enough
And I couldn't go down with you

I've seen too many bloody arms
Too many rows of scars
And I never thought love could be so fucking hard

The pain had become a drug
Back before you started smoking weed
Back when it was you and me
But if we're being honest it was always just me
Because you were so out of it that you weren't really there

I was your girlfriend
Not your babysitter
And I know you felt guilty for making me into one
But guilt's not enough when I'll spend the rest of my life
Scared to put down my phone
Or close my eyes

poetry

Don't wanna be what pushes you over the edge
I can't stay
But I can't leave

poetry

POUCH OF LAVENDER

EMMA MIRNICS

Grade 12. Millard North High School, Omaha, NE. Joshua Lingenfelter, Educator. *Honorable Mention.*

Portfolio Gold Key

Alone,
hangs a bundle of nothing but dried herbs wrapped in cloth and purple lace,
soft when first touched,
yet it crackles when pressed, and the grainy texture abounds from beneath the blanket,
along with shriveled leaves, leaking through pores of cloth and pricking fingers.
Now dangling from its ribbon like leaves on a willow,
emitting a sweet aroma, a band of calm that expands throughout the room.
To some it serves as uplifting freedom from stress,
But to others, the scent carries nostalgia, transporting the soul
back to the place of its origin, a place far across the Atlantic
on the Adriatic Coast with waves battering a rocky shore and the taste of salty air,

poetry

all so vastly different, yet still the same for the omnipresent fragrance
in a time that had once been.
Now, dangling from its ribbon like leaves on a willow,
on it embroidered "Croatia," condemning it to be a souvenir.
Alone,
it hangs, mainly ignored or forgotten
But every now and then, whispering, "moje srce," *my heart,*
a reminder of the relatives left behind in distant lands,
as if Americans would let immigrants forget their accents,
forget that despite thirty years in America,
despite starting a family,
despite acquiring citizenship,
this country is not their home.
Alone,
Gently swinging under the fan,
Now singing louder, "kako lijepo," *how pretty,*
To have the strength to escape a war
To build a better life through the hard work only immigrants know
To radiate glowing hope through a gift of lavender
prevailing through the smiles of their children.

Home, Peace of the Season

Emma Mirnics

Grade 12. Millard North High School, Omaha, NE. Joshua Lingenfelter, Educator. *Honorable Mention.*

Portfolio Gold Key

Home

Dilapidated ceilings, crumbling walls
Sunny skies, open windows
Rotting barns, wild garden
Crowing rooster, noisy chickens

Baka says "Dobro jutro," *good morning,*
as I come down the stairs for breakfast
My grandmother loves more than most,
even if her pride won't let her show it.

My uncle acknowledges that they have less,
But here in Croatia, they have their pride, and rightfully so,
Because the people of my heritage have so much more.

Bolja hrana, *better food,*
Bolji nogomet, *better soccer,*
Bolji zivot, *better life.*

poetry

Time slows down in Baka's village, Daruvar.
The war may have aged the buildings, still riddled with
bullet holes,
and the people, now elderly in years,
but the war did not take away their way of life.

Love here is expressed through food and religious
tokens,
as Baka teaches me to bake kiflice, *rolls,*
and buys me my eleventh rosary and a bottle of holy
water.
We sit on the porch, sipping sok od bazge, *elderflower
juice,*
idly chatting with the neighbors about all the problems
of the world.

I wonder what my American friends would think if
they saw me here,
Here, with my family, who have known hardship and
persevered
Here, with the people who have worked harder and
longer than most,
Here, with the people who know all their neighbors'
life stories,
Here, with the people who leave their doors and opin-
ions unlocked.

With all the luxuries and opportunities built by a new
life,
my home and my heart are in America.

But with all the honesty and ease of an intimate way of
life,
my home and my heart are here with my heritage and
family in Hrvatska, *Croatia*.

Peace of the Season

The sunshine couldn't taste any sweeter
Fulfilling warmth, but not burning or stifling
The breeze breathing life into my aching soul
At last enveloping my spirit in nourishing peace
The fallen leaves of hope cast into the air once more
Painting the air with a saturated crispness of colors
The sun setting over summer
Calling out to the autumn moon

I am a mere member of this exclusive club of life
swathed in the first icy wind
This burgeoning world is mine
and I belong to its sky
These creamy clouds surging
over the pale pink mist of a new season
There is a palpable buzz racing towards the unknown
while I remain slow and deliberate

steadily rising toward the waning light
As the orb dips from my perception
I can't help but feel the vibrations inside
calling out
We will disappear together

poetry

Epilogue, Epilogue II

Elise Vahle

Grade 12. Grand Island Senior High School, Grand Island, NE. Jerome Dubas, Educator. *Honorable Mention.*

Epilogue

See, the issue with memories is that,
despite two people experiencing the same events,
we can remember them completely different

I remember you as both an extended metaphor and an unwritten letter
The silences were always worse than the elaboration
But we both know how you bottle everything up,
a castaway stuck on your own personal timebomb island
The longer you stay there, the more severe the damages hit you
The extended metaphor of you goes like this: I'm still writing it
and you've still extended to my present day, no matter how I try to repress you
You're a lump in my throat, and a stone in my stomach
like the ones you forced me to swallow

poetry

to keep this frail figment from floating away
Those stones still remain, battered and bruised organs
along with them
More or less, you still remain
Your blank page letters still haunt me
and oh how I wish I could defuse your damage,
I most certainly tried
But I guess I had more than enough of my own at the
time

I remember you like a dog remembers an electric
fence,
"*I never want to stumble across that again*"

Epilogue II

Perhaps, the problem with forgetting things is you
must remember them first
I don't think I can do that without driving the stake in
further
I'll ignore the bleeding until the drips become a metro-
nome, keeping time with the beating of my heart

Simply put—though you know I've never been sim-
ple—I am numb to you
I let thoughts evaporate like soaked cotton t-shirts in
the summer sun
How they once stuck to my body,

poetry

a second skin I couldn't shake away
but I didn't let it harden
You were never an outer shell, how I hate the fact that
at one time you thought that
I was only a husk without you

I don't remember the circles your fingertips traced on
my back, like a written language you curated and
only we spoke
I don't remember the brown of your eyes, how you
hated the color but all I could see in them were
forgotten forest trails waiting to be trekked
I don't remember your rule of threes, how everything
worthwhile comes in triplets
I don't *still* use it when I write about you

All I can wish for is a bookmark, so I can leave this
chapter for a while but not forget my place
I don't remember wishing to think about you again
Perhaps that's why I can't forget

Collateral Damage

Jingming Yu

Grade 11. East High School, Lincoln, NE. Sarah Staples-Farmer, Educator. *Honorable Mention.*

Strange woman,
Always sat on the pink bed in the living room of my
grandparents' apartment,
Dead but alive,
The smiles were angelic but the words slurred
Like a maple syrup of a confusing flavor,
One that I'm too young to tolerate.

On the table was always a plate of fruit,
Four different melons you needed to scoop the meat of
with a spoon.
I should eat but I am enraptured,
Your charm, the enigma of you,
Your syrup language I distrust was your first.

We were connected yet apart
By these land masses on opposite sides of this blue
marble
When I entered you left,
Only briefly, an exchange,

poetry

And in exchange for the briefness is the permanence of
our settlement.
Unintentional was the collateral,
An almost united family in exchange for your mind,
Splintered in an eight-month sleep.

Was it unsafe to cross the winding road?
Were they moving so quick that it was hard to see,
A traffic rush,
Sped up videos of cars driving along highways,
But in real time,
Leaving streamers of lights,
So easy to dance into,
Slipping between the curtains.

I only knew you after,
Strange woman,
Now gone,
The car but a fraction of many,
Collided collateral.
A punishment for a dream.

Tomorrow

Elizabeth Grantham

Grade 12. Westside High School, Omaha, NE. Liz Hough, Educator. *Gold Key. American Voices Nominee.*

The shattered flower vase glared up at Jessica from the filthy kitchen floor and she wondered if it was silently mocking her. That'd be pretty rude of it if it was. After all, that vase had been her absolute favorite, a gift from her late mother, actually, and watching it break into a million pieces broke her heart in nearly the exact same way.

She guessed it was kind of her fault. She had left it on the very edge of the counter, meaning to put fresh tulips in it later, and Randy, needing the nearest available thing to throw at his younger sister, had grabbed it. Which is how it broke. It had also bruised Elena's forehead, but Jessica wasn't too worried about that because the forehead would eventually fix itself. The flower vase, however, would not.

She sighed and reached for the broom and dustpan, which were trapped under the giant box of Victoria's Secret magazines her husband had so carelessly decided to set on top of them. Briefly, Jessica wondered if her children might be willing to come help move it,

flash fiction

but then decided not to ask, remembering how things turned out the *last* time she wanted them to do something for her.

So, instead, Jessica managed to lift the box all by herself, grabbed the broom and dustpan from underneath it, and then quickly set to work, sweeping the broken shards into a pile. From downstairs, she could hear Randy and Elena watching TV together, more likely than not enjoying one of the R-rated movies their father liked to screen every now and then. Of course, *she* didn't want her children to see *any* R-rated films, but there was only so much she could do since Alexander let them watch pretty much whatever they wanted, no matter how inappropriate it might be for them.

Besides, the TV kept them quiet. Jessica wished it didn't, but it did, and having *something* that managed to keep her children from fighting was better than having nothing at all. She smirked, suddenly finding the whole thing amusing. How quickly her kids' behavior had changed once she told them to go watch TV instead of clean the kitchen! One minute they were trying to kill each other and the next, they were the best of friends. Technology really did work miracles.

Jessica straightened up and cracked her neck, carefully dumping the dustpan into the trash can as she did so. The shards clinked against the metal walls, like some sort of hellish solo, and she sighed for the second time that day. That really had been her favorite vase. Maybe not her most beautiful, but definitely her favorite. It had reminded her of the life she once led, a life that was now nothing more than a fading memory and a handful of broken glass in the garbage can. Such a crying shame, really. And such an unfortunate regret as well.

"Stop that," Jessica told herself angrily, while mentally pouring a bucket of cold water over herself. "Quit thinking so negatively. Sure, things didn't go so well today, but everyone has days like that. Tomorrow will be different. Tomorrow will be just fine. Tomorrow will be better, you'll see!"

Nobody answered her. Her phone started to ring, but she didn't bother picking it up since it was probably just Alexander telling her he was going to have to stay late at work again. The TV continued to quietly mumble from downstairs and the broom and dustpan stood as stiff and still as ever. The flower vase lay broken in the bottom of the trashcan, but for whatever reason, Jessica thought it was silently laughing at her.

Adele's Introduction

Aila Hirsbrunner

Grade 12. Lincoln Southwest High School, Lincoln, NE. Donald Strasheim, Educator. *Silver Key.*

Moldy, muddy water lines the brick walls of the surrounding buildings of the alley.

"Hello, little miss," a laughing voice calls to me. The man is smoking something that smells bad. He has on a dark brown jacket and loose blue jeans. His face is scruffy, homeless like. All complete with mismatching winter hat and gloves with holes at the fingers. I walk faster past him and put my eyes to the ground, doing everything to avoid him.

A door appears a few feet from me. I pull it, hard, remembering how my father did so many years ago. Cell phones and laptops stock the shelves of the shop.

"What can I do for you, little lady?" the shopkeeper asks.

"Dust Bunny." That was the last thing my father said to me.

"You don't happen to be Ben's little girl, do ya'?" he asks, handing me the cell phone my father gave him for safekeeping.

"Ya."

"Welp, be careful. You can't be going on in the rebellion with a kid," he says, nodding his head at my stomach.

"I don't plan on going in the rebellion."

"Still, this world isn't safe for a child. Be careful, Adele." I nod and walk back through the door, shoving the phone in my backpack.

I walk past signs saying, "Possession of Technology Will Lead to 50 Years in Prison" and "Too Much Tech Equals Death." The government says technology "ruined" our nation back in 2036. The democracy we had is slowly turning more and more into a dictatorship. There is a rebellion, though. Everyone in it has to cover up their face and hair. If the government finds out who they are, they'll put them on the militia's list.

The militia is a government-funded, government-led organization that goes out each night and kills whoever is on their list (the government claims to have no part in this whatsoever). The list is given to the militia by the government. Some on their list are part of the rebellion, and some aren't. It's set up to scare people. My father made sure I knew all about the militia. He would say things like, "Honey, I'll die from the militia, but you, you will soar. I'll make sure of it."

I am his successor, whether I like it or not. No one here is happy; we're all afraid of being killed by the militia. But my husband, Cody, and I were doing fine. High school sweethearts, marriage, and on to the next stage of our lives, parenthood. But, along with my father, Cody was on the militia's same list. Now, if I want my son to grow up in a better world, I have to change it. I have to finish my father's work.

flash fiction

THE TEARS FALL TOO

MALIK GILLESPIE

Grade 12. Westside High School, Omaha, NE. Liz Hough, Educator. *Honorable Mention.*

Portfolio Silver Key

"Do you think the Devil cried when he fell?" the boy asked. He was small, barely old enough to face the struggle of growing facial hair, yet the world had apparently decided that he was old enough to face the struggle of surviving a place like this.

"I think—" The man spoke up, the high ceiling of the small room adding a slight echo to the words. His voice hid his fear very well but not his sadness. His face was streaked with tears, glistening in the light of the rising sun like liquid crystals. Guilt and grief were old friends, and it showed; their stories were carved in the scars of his body, stitched into his skin to weave a patchwork masterpiece of pain out of his body. "I think the only time the Devil cried was after he fell."

"Did it hurt?" the boy asked. He went closer to the window, looking at the ground far below. The city—or rather, what remains of it—was usually avoided by the scavengers of their community. It was dangerous; they

flash fiction

were lawless. No-man's-land. Back in the days before, that was a term used for war zones, a place claimed by neither side. It fits now too, except there are no sides but one's own, and the war is over—in a sense, at least. It might be more accurate to say a war will always be ongoing, even if it had been a different and larger war that left the planet and its people plunged into desolation. "It must've hurt to fall so far."

The man doesn't say much, just looks past the boy at the rubble of the city. He wasn't very old himself, but he was old enough to remember. Sometimes, he wonders if he's too old to hope in this world. "Yeah, I think it did."

What isn't said is that it wasn't the fall that hurt most, it was being alone afterward. The man had wondered, just after he had survived the world ending, if loneliness is what made the devil a monster; if being cast out by all he had known hurt more than landing among the unknown. In the ruins of the world, the people like him—the ones unlucky enough to have survived with the memories of the past—know loss like one knows an infection. An invader of their bodies and minds, leaving behind the taste of regret and blood both.

"I hope he feels better now," the boy says. This is the difference between the ones who remember and the ones who don't know anything besides this word; the ones who don't have a "before," only a "now." The ones like the boy know laughter and can keep going in ways the ones like the man don't. They are all surrounded by remnants of a world they can never go back to, but only the ones like the man are tortured by their own memories. "I think even the devil wants to rest."

"I think so too," the man said. The new generation knows how to find hope in the debris and peace in the ravages because they were not forged while the world was burning; they rose while the world was falling. Like the devil, they too got up again after the fall.

BANG

AILA HIRSBRUNNER

Grade 12. Lincoln Southwest High School, Lincoln, NE. Donald Strasheim, Educator. *Honorable Mention.*

A young couple walks into a coffee shop. BANG BANG. "Run!" "I'm at the Teargate Mall." BANG. "My baby!" BANG BANG. "People are screaming all around me." "I assure you, sir, the police are on their way." BANG. The two watch the news lady fail at beating the other sounds her camera picks up on the TV.

"You'll be fine," the girl says.

"How can you be so sure?" the boy asks, confused.

"You're smart and really good at thinking out-of-the-box."

"Really?"

"Yeah. You'll definitely make it out alive."

The two get to the counter.

"A Caramel Brulee Latte, please," the girl says eagerly.

"Uh, I'll just have a lemonade."

"But what about you?" the boy continues.

"Hopefully, I'm never in that situation."

"Well, what if you were?"

"I'd die, of course."

"Here you go." The lady behind the counter slides their drinks to the couple.

"What if I saved you?" he asks, catching up to her.

"Then you'd be my hero," she laughs.

The two sit down next to a window. One across from the other. "Cell phones on the table," the girl reminds him and sets hers down in the middle.

"I'm serious," he says, putting his phone on top of hers. "What would you do if it happened right here and now?"

"I'd follow you," she says. "Or I'd kill myself."

"What?! Why?"

"I'd kill myself if I got in your way."

"You wouldn't get in my way."

"Yeah I would. I don't have any survival skills like you do."

"Even if, why kill yourself?"

"Because, if I get in your way too much, you could die."

"We both could die at any moment in time. What's your point?"

The girl turns her head to the side and stares out the window. "Never mind. Drink your lemonade."

Silence takes them now. The boy occupies his time by watching the TV and the girl looks out the window. She sees a few dogs pass by, and birds rest on a power line across the street. On the TV the screaming continues. The BANGs continue. All like there's no end.

"Would you really save me?" the girl asks.

"I hope so. I don't know what my instincts would have me do," the boy responds. "I might even freeze. Then you'd have to take the lead," he jokes.

To Fall to Rise

Emma Mirnics

Grade 12. Millard North High School, Omaha, NE. Joshua Lingenfelter, Educator. *Gold Key. American Voices Nominee.*

Portfolio Gold Key

Treacherous was the climb down to the village in the canyon. Nessie Bright and her team of mountaineers spent days descending the rocky wall into the small town of Caldera. As they took their first steps on the ground, the valley they had heard so much about assaulted their senses.

It was a little before sunset, but Caldera was already dark. The surrounding mountains loomed around the village from all sides, effectively cutting off any direct sunlight, imposing a veil of shade at all hours. Looking around, the lack of sunshine had clearly taken its toll on the barren patch of earth they had arrived to. Nessie and her team paused to wonder what set of events had brought them to this place at this moment.

The villagers, at first ignorant, eventually took notice of the newcomers' arrival and assembled to greet

short story

them. An old man was the first to approach them. "Welcome to Caldera," he exclaimed, "your new home!"

"Oh no—we're just passing through," Nessie responded.

"That's what we all think at first! But everyone who comes, stays," he winked.

"So," Nessie scanned the crowd before gathering her thoughts, "you like it here?" This question elicited a chorus of bitter-sounding laughs and chuckles from the crowd.

"No! Of course not. Would you look at this place? Who could ever love it here? It's just that the cliffs are too steep to climb," the old man told her.

"No, there has to be a mistake," Nessie assured him. "We just came down the cliffs, and I know we can climb them easily. They're really only steep hills," Nessie told him, but as she looked up at the way from which she came, suddenly the hills seemed taller, steeper, and slicker. She began to question if perhaps the old man was right.

"It's too dangerous. I'll get out one day though. I have too many things left to do to stay here," the old man promised Nessie.

"So why don't you? Leave, I mean?" asked Nessie.

"Because the walls are too high and too steep! Surely you can see that. Look!" The old man pointed. As Nessie spun around studying the imposing cliffs, she saw that he was indeed telling the truth. There was no way any of them could climb their way out.

"This is ridiculous! I'm leaving first thing in the morning, and Nessie, guys, I assume you're all coming with me," interrupted Frank Jefferson, a member of Nessie's team.

"Frank, I don't know that you can. Look at the cliffs. They're too high and too steep, just as this man says," replied Nessie. "Perhaps we better get used to it down here." Nessie did not intend on staying in Caldera, but her eyes had finally been opened to the fact that it was impossible to climb out.

The old man gently coughed, his cue to rejoin the conversation. "I'll take you to an empty house by mine and get you acquainted to your new permanent residence." The band of mountaineers shared glances with each other as they followed the old man, politely easing their pace to match his slow and labored strides. "Something about the air up here can make everything difficult," he remarked. As soon as he mentioned it, Nessie began to feel the heaviness herself, and in no time she found it hard to keep up with the old man at all.

The group finally arrived at two gray structures. Nessie understood these to be the houses, but they were dilapidated and unfeeling. She supposed that there must have been underlying colors in the paint and paneling, but every broken element was overshadowed by the same gray veil. Even more peculiar, Nessie realized that neither of the structures had windows. As she glanced around at the rest of the village, she noticed all of the buildings looked the same as these: gray and windowless.

Frank spoke aloud that which the others wouldn't dare. "These look absolutely miserable. How can you stay in these things? There's no way any of this is remotely comfortable, or even bearable!"

The old man looked at Frank as a teacher looks at a child and told him, "That's what we all think at first, but you'll find that you really don't mind. You'll get used to it in no time." He opened the door to an inside grayer than the outside, ushering the mountaineers inside.

Nessie studied the walls and the old man's face. She saw that he was once again speaking the truth. The sight she initially thought repugnant was now not so bad at all. She picked out a gray bedroom, claiming it as her own. Although she was convinced she wouldn't be staying, since she couldn't climb out, she decided to settle in.

The old man left them, bidding them goodnight with a promise to return early the next day. He warned them that they wouldn't sleep but told them not to concern themselves with such a trivial matter. As Nessie closed her eyes, she found that sleep never came. Lying in bed, she found herself sinking into the mattress with its board stabbing her skin like sand-covered rocks, but as the old man suggested, she decided to pay no attention to the prickly sensations keeping her conscious in the dark.

Eventually time passed, and while there was no increase in light, the whole house stirred, collectively understanding it to be morning. Surely enough, as they exited the structure, the old man was waiting for them.

"Alright well thank you for your hospitality, but we should really be going now, right guys?" asked Frank.

Nessie looked at Frank curiously. "Frank, we can't," she said. "It's too steep and too slick to climb." The other mountaineers nodded in agreement with her, all having come to the same conclusion.

"Suit yourselves. I'm leaving right now. It's time for me to continue with my life," Frank told them, shouldering his gear and heading to the closest cliff. Sure enough, Nessie and the group watched him as he began to climb, and Nessie found doubt grow in her new convictions. Perhaps she was right the first time; perhaps the climb could be done after all.

"Come. Let us go and face the day," said the old man. He led them to a gray stream where the other villagers had already gathered, each with their own place along the shore. Gray shrubs waved their gray branches with their shimmering gray leaves, all gently waving at the same slow pace as the water they guarded. The stream was like no other creek that Nessie had ever seen. The water seemed to crawl, and instead of a gentle rushing sound, its delicate movements projected sounds like whispers.

"I will leave you now to become familiar with the people of Caldera," the old man said. They watched as he took his own place along the shore, closing his eyes and growing deathly still.

A nearby woman approached Nessie and asked her, "What will you do when you leave Caldera?"

"Well, I suppose I had always planned to climb Everest!" Nessie replied. "What about you?"

The woman spared a smile before telling her tale. She said, "I'm an engineer, and I'm going to build the rocket that gets astronauts to Mars."

As Nessie walked from neighbor to neighbor, asking each of them of their plans, each was grander than the next. A teenager aspired to be president, her ponytail bobbing with her words as she spoke. An elderly scientist promised to eradicate cancer, talking in tones that could only be likened to the sounds of the stream. A grizzled lawyer proposed a solution for a more just system. If only the walls weren't too high and too steep.

Nessie couldn't help but wonder how all these people got here. Many of them were young, but even the smallest couldn't have been any younger than thirteen. Nessie also saw an astonishing number of elderly folk, but she couldn't tell if they had been here all this time or if they had simply just arrived.

The shadows seemed to shift as the hidden sun snaked across the sky while Nessie drifted from conversation to conversation. She glanced up at the cliffs and saw Frank's red backpack visible about a third of the way up from the base of the mountain. At once, Nessie felt an inexplicable surge of energy, and she ran to the old man.

"Look! Look how far Frank made it! That initial section is by far the slipperiest. It's not too dangerous after all. We can leave and get on with our lives!" she exclaimed.

The old man looked at her with an omniscient smile. "Who are you talking about? I neither see to whom you are pointing nor understand to whom you are referring. No one leaves Caldera. The walls are too high and too steep." Nessie peered back at the cliff and at once had trouble finding Frank's red backpack among the rocks. She began to wonder if he had even existed at all.

"Don't worry. It's normal to see such things when you first arrive, but sooner or later you'll understand the impossibility." Nessie saw that the old man was right as always, so she promised herself to be more conscientious in the future. "Now it is time that you find your own place here, where you can spend your days.

Wander these banks and stop where the air feels heaviest. This is how you will know you belong."

Without moving, Nessie knew that the spot on which she stood would be the heaviest she would ever feel, so she planted herself firmly whispering, "Here." The old man left her and returned to the place he initially stood motionless and presumably resumed his prior ponderings.

Nessie did not have to be told what to do anymore. It was as if her body was programmed to know the next series of actions. She closed her eyes and allowed instinct to take over. Her body grew still, and her eyes fell shut. She felt the chill of Caldera pinching every part of her, inside and out as the heaviness pressed down. Then all at once, the sound of the river began to empty her out. The overwhelming nothingness consumed her. Her mind neither thought nor felt; the emptiness simply became her. The peculiar sensation was neither pleasant nor painful. The sensation was nothing itself. She was neither aware of the breeze, nor the gentle whispers trickling to her ears from upstream. Nessie retreated into herself, enveloped within the world within her mind, as it hollowed itself out into oblivion.

By the time Nessie opened her eyes again, it was well past dark. Rather than stumble to find her way back to the gray house, she decided to spend the night here at the river. It was in this moment that Nessie realized

Caldera was the same. No matter where she might go, every part of the village was identical in every measure. Most villagers had left the river, but a couple others like her had stayed. Some still stood while others had lain down to rest. The coarse river rocks needled her, but Nessie chose to sleep anyway, this time successfully losing consciousness.

When Nessie awoke, she opened her eyes to the sound of screaming. Whose screams they were, she did not know. Caldera had been good to her, but Nessie's bubble of doubt was threatening to pop, expanding within her like a balloon being blown up by an overzealous child. The place that she was ready to call her home, while friendly, seemed wrong. Nessie was missing something, something that sent worms crawling across her skin.

Caldera this morning seemed exceptionally misty, and Nessie soon discovered that this mist, like a dense fog, was a rather permanent feature of Caldera. Months passed, and Nessie found that she had trouble recalling anything other than the omnipresent haze and her hours spent retreating within herself by the whispering stream.

One morning, after almost four months spent as a citizen of her new residency, was different. The sun rose at such an angle to just barely be visible, casting its light on a particular cliff. As Nessie traced the path of the sunbeam with her eyes, she saw it. Frank's red backpack at the top. Had he come back to Caldera? With the limited energy Nessie could muster, she stumbled to the old man to tell him the news of Frank's success.

He was there, Nessie could see him. Frank was there, waiting for her at the top of the cliff. She was ready to leave Caldera. Passing through had already passed too much of her life away, so Nessie decided she would climb. She turned to the old man, telling him, "I'm going to try climbing the walls. I hope you'll come with me."

The old man looked cruel in the early morning light as he vehemently affirmed, "Climbing out is impossible. You cannot do it, and you will never leave Caldera."

With that, Nessie's doubts suddenly clouded her head once more, telling her that the old man was right, but this time, she would not cave in so easily. Shaking her head and shouldering her gear, Nessie headed to the cliff she saw Frank peering over, his bright red backpack a sun against the grayness of the village.

Nessie knew the hardest part of the climb would be the start. She did not think it was possible, but in her heart of hearts, Nessie decided she would try. With one hand reaching out, and one leg stepping up, Nessie began to lift herself onto the rocks. Her mind was telling her this was easy for her, or at least it should have been, but she kept hearing the old man's voice telling her she could not do it. His words found their way to her hands, to her toes, and to the core that kept her attached to the mountain. Fingers that had never shaken before began to tremble, and muscles that had never failed before began to weaken. All the same, Nessie was going to try.

Hand after hand, lunge after lunge, Nessie could feel herself rising. Though she was progressing, she dared not look down. Though her body knew the way, the old man's voice started screaming.

The dark cloud of night started creeping in just as Nessie spotted an awning where she decided she would sleep. And with each labored breath, Nessie knew though her panting grew heavier, her burden grew lighter. Each step was a weight released. Once safely on the ledge, she stole a glance downward, at last acknowledging how far she had come.

As Nessie reached the top of the mountain, she at last pulled herself up, smiling with her face pressed towards the sun. She looked around, searching for Frank, who had come back for her, before realizing that it was not Frank who had rescued her. After so much time relying on the voices of others, Nessie knew the truth. She had left Caldera by herself.

Sparing a final glance down at the village below her, Nessie's heart rejoiced when she saw the teenager, Elissa, who so many months ago had spoken of her aspirations to be president, beginning the climb up the cliff.

RUST

ELLEN PAN

Grade 9. East High School, Lincoln, NE. Francesca Rohrs, Educator. *Silver Key.*

Some people say that you can't smell anything when you were asleep. Is that true? It must be, because the first thing I sensed every morning, as my body pulled itself from rest, was not the fluttering of my eyes or the blankets over my skin, but the blatant scent of rust that I had never known was gone until it returned. Try to pretend that you never awoke and drift back to welcome sleep—try—but it won't work. No man can *pretend* he doesn't acknowledge the rust. It slowly spreads, down, down into your lungs and from there seeps into your blood, until you feel like an old statue rotting away in unheard ruins.

It stayed like that for a while.

And then my eyes fluttered open, my skin thawed to acknowledge the linty blankets draped over my body, my ears ceased their high-pitched ringing, and I was awake.

short story

You might ask where I lived. You might wonder if there was some way that you could lend a helping hand—but no, if you're reading this, I'm afraid that you're very far in the past, living in a glorious fun-time world. I can tell you now, if you'd care to listen—enjoy the good days when war is not blooming in your eyes, when rancid meat isn't a thing more sacred than gold. Please, I beg you, watch every rise and fall of the stars, drink all your fresh water, breathe like there's no air to come tomorrow—it's a luxury. Cherish every moment of *having* until you don't. Trust me, there's no better raconteur than I.

How should I tell you about the downfall of our world?

I blinked once. Outside the window, inky black clouds boiled in the sky like restless beasts ready to feed. Winds gasped shuddering breaths; the air grew hotter and heavier with each passing second. It felt as if we were eternally draped under a thick, wooly blanket, childhood's fort-building play welded into reality.

I looked over at Grandma, whose tiny, hunched silhouette was still shrouded with sleep. Soon she would wake up.

Today, blue smoke burned out the horizon, making the whole world a blended stretch of fumes. It was more than yesterday; red silhouettes of decaying skyscrapers twisted and turned in the wafting smog like dancing giants at our demise. When would anything be better? I always prayed for tomorrow, though there was no strength or reason to hope for it. Getting through today was hard enough.

You're asking why I lived in such a terrible place. World War IV—you don't know about that, surely. You don't hear murmurs on the streets about its dawn just yet. Maybe it's centuries away from your time, maybe just a decade or two. But for now, you're living in a prosperous world where hunger and thirst are the least of worries to you. World War IV changed a lot of things; it inevitably shattered families, tore them apart into irretrievable pieces. It also ceased all thoughts of happiness and, with pain, gave birth to the world I walked now.

Grandma often told me stories about the war. She spoke of bombs that flew shrieking through the air like sleek birds, eating up an island with each strike. All the grand culture, accumulated through centuries of sweat and glory, grew abandoned as more blood was shed and less ran warm in live bodies. To those who had fallen, rust soon lay his delicate tentacles around their neck and from then on seized the crumbling world.

Oh, the rust was everywhere. It was in our food, our water, our clothes and hair and skin. Great big drifts of it were stripped from ancient architecture every minute, sent by the wind high into the sky, only to snow down upon us once more. Rust flew into our mouth every time we spoke, plastered to the roof and wedged between the teeth. I had wasted countless precious liquids in failed attempts to spit it out, only to admit defeat at last. But most of all was the terrible, terrible scent that it emanated at an ambitious goal to stain the entire world. No water would wash away the blood-like rust which clung to our nostrils like relentless perfume.

Tell me about your time. Is it truly like Grandma told me? She spoke of airplanes like enormous birds that could lift beyond the clouds, tiny pieces of glass that you could put to your ear and talk to anyone anywhere, and the Internet, which was an invisible ghost who knew everything. She told me about how beautiful the architecture once was, gleaming silver skyscrapers leaping out of torn earth like magnificent giants. She told me that they could reach into the sky, poke a hole through that thin dome of blue and let all the stars fall into the world.

There was a long, shuddering sigh that melted into the groaning winds as Grandma pulled herself from the floor, now awake. Her blue eyes opened in a mass of wrinkles and turned to me. She had a way of smiling through her eyes without her wrinkled, toothless mouth ever flinching, which I had practiced many times before the mirror but could never master.

Grandma was a raconteur of sorts, I liked to think. She was the only person that I knew who was born under a blue sky and drew her first breath with clean air welcoming her lungs to the world. Like a raconteur, she survived the twelve years of hope-drenching war, stooped with age, and lived to pass her stories on to the next generation.

"Tell me a story," I said, when she had sat up. The mornings always began with a story of the past, so that I could gather up enough courage to face the present.

Grandma's eyes crinkled into another subtle smile. I couldn't help but try it myself, though I suspected that my expression was nowhere near pleasant. When she opened her ancient mouth to speak, I imagined her drawing a memory from beneath the silvery-white hair.

"Well ... you've heard every one of them. I've been tellin' you stories since you were a baby that knew not how to speak yourself. Let me repeat and refine my stories then, for I'm quite afraid that my blunt old memory had left out a few good details—" She stopped to clear her throat as a magician did before his final act.

"The sun is a bright copper thing, hangin' there in the sky," she began. The way Grandma spoke was mysterious, like words of ink scratched on cracked yellow parchment. "I like to think that the sun is an eye of the sky. Is there a place where

short story

the sunlight can't reach? Even the darkest shadows have no defense against her, and so the sun is an eye that knows all."

Grandma had a way of dropping her g's unexpectedly at the end of each word and elongating each vowel that exited her lips. I always thought that it was an accent from the old days, and I liked it. It had a bit of a lazy feel to it that reminded me of sleep and the smell of wet sand.

"But the sun never made her appearance after the first gunshot of World War IV. You should have seen her, dear. She made a grand flight every day over the sky, so that you could marvel at her full splendor without end. The sun lavished a coat of buttery light over everything, before her bright eye was clouded by all this smoke."

Beautiful as her story was, I knew that this one was a lie. You know it too—about the ice-blue sky and cotton-candy clouds, a heaven compared to this smoggy waste outside my window, but there was no such thing as the *sun*. A tall, dancing bonfire couldn't pierce through darkness more than a few feet away, so how could anything be bright enough to light up the whole world for hours without ever flickering out? And if the sun truly did close her eye below the western horizon, how could she wake again on the eastern lands? Tell me how anything could be powerful enough to bleed the entire sky a cocktail of purple and gold within a single blink of the eye. No, not even the gods had that sort of power. War must have seeped into Grandma's head, must have painted a story on her tongue that was too beautiful to be true.

Grandma had told me many stories, some sensible and some outright absurd. I knew that the architecture was real, for I lived in the hollows of their corpses myself. You must be reading my story in one of those buildings right now. Tell me, are their walls truly as sleek and shiny as captured moonlight? Do the tall glass windows catch prisms of the rainbow and reflect them onto the earth? Perhaps you're living in the same apartment as I did thousands of years later. In your time, you would witness the skyscrapers growing way into the clouds to poke swirling holes in the ice-blue sky, and watch as thousands upon thousands of stars make their descent from heaven. Now, eras later, the buildings had long shed their glamour as dead crows shed their feathers, and they swayed like summertime drunks in the tongues of wind. It was eerie how much they resembled soldiers lost in the stampede of war, with nothing left on their raw skin but layer upon layer of rust.

Was rust not meant to be a symbol of the dead and gone? The devil was known to lay his slender, red fingers only upon forgotten things. Yet it grew everywhere, climbing upon whatever surface they could grasp. Huge mounds of it spewed across the streets so that we stood knee-deep in rust every day. The awful red bleached its way into everything, until no one could speak with certainty of another free, untainted color. There was no rainfall to cleanse us—even the gods had turned their backs and refused to weep for our predicament.

All this was caused by World War IV, a strangling fight between the Earth and its inhabitants that dragged on for twelve whole years.

"The smoke of war had blotted out the sun, true, but the real fight had begun centuries ago, far back ... in the second era, I'd say. People before us—that's my ancestors, and yours—they built all of the prosperity that I lived in. But beautiful as it was, they had offended Mother Earth. She wasn't respected after all that she's given—her gold, her silver, iron, all taken away from beneath her skin in the worst way. Our ancestors lavished resources, and from there, centuries later, World War IV was finally born. No one won, of course. The only result was the destruction of Mother Earth. We took so much from her that she's bleeding now, bleeding all that rust that used to be beautiful iron, kept safe under her skin. Look at the rust. Do you see how much it's like blood? My ancestors and yours did this to her. The guilt runs in my blood, May. The guilt runs in your blood too.

"Finally there came a time when Mother Earth began to weep. Her tears fell into the seas, and they rose so high that they gulped up France, China, Egypt—those are big

short story

countries, but along with them her tears drowned countless others as well. Have you tasted a tear before? The sea is salty just like that."

Grandma never told me how she knew all of this. I thought that neither of us really knew anything about the world outside of America; most of her stories were probably feverish dreams. I didn't even know if there was a world outside of America. I didn't know if France or China or Egypt were real countries.

But Grandma was right about one thing. Mother Earth was never meant to be exploited in this fashion: all her riches, carefully painted into shape and preserved for eras on, dug up within years by coughing excavators and used to decorate the painful, sparkling crown of cities that she wore atop her head. Oils that made vehicles run turned crisp winds into labored gasps. When oil ceased, my ancestors chopped down trees; when trees no longer grew, they broke into war. When the war ended, Mother Earth was nothing more than an echoing corpse, spoiled with her own blood.

Are you one of my ancestors? The time that you're living in, does Mother Earth have any more to offer? I'm quite afraid that if there is, there isn't much left. The glamorous world that you see constructing before you, all the neon cityscapes, they come with a price.

A sandstorm was starting to gather outside, blurring the spidery red giants for a moment. Grandma wrapped a scarf around her head; I put a ragged blanket over my nose and went to the corner to join her.

Grandma began her story once more, her ancient, wrinkly voice muffled by the scarf. Her blue eyes were showing, the only things in the world that weren't bleached red with rust. They had not aged one bit since the good times, never dimmed from looking at the raging gray sky. Sitting there, I could almost imagine that Grandma was a young woman, sapphire-like eyes still filled with hope. But then she extended her withered hand to hold mine, and the imagination evaporated.

"Before the sea had filled up with Earth's tears, it was the most beautiful thing in the world. It's the biggest mirror, blue in the day and silver in the night—oh, how I wish you could see it for yourself."

"And it's made out of water?" I asked. The sea was another thing that I didn't believe existed. No matter how hard I tried, I couldn't bring to my eyes a picture of water, just an endless expanse of water that stretched to the edge of the world and on. I had never seen a pool bigger than the size of my hand before.

Grandma shook a little bit with laughter. "Oh, indeed it is! All water, stretching for miles and miles on. I've heard sailors say that it took months to get across the ocean, that's how big it is. And the waves! I've seen them with my own two eyes, when I was a young girl like you. Terrific monsters, they rise up ten feet high in the air, maybe more."

I didn't believe her words. Here it scarcely rained once a year, and when it did, the rain was bitter like bile. There could not possibly be a place in the world where one could be fully submerged in water and not see the bottom, much less miles of it. If there was, we wouldn't be suffering cracked lips and dry throats.

The sandstorm grew bolder as it lashed out full-blast on us, swaying our dingy apartment like it was a ridiculous snow globe. Grit hid beneath my tongue and between my lashes, while more and more rust shook from its boundaries and flew away. Mother Earth was drawing up her final howl, unleashing her ultimate rage. I thought of yesterday, when the storms were half as severe, and I had prayed for a better tomorrow. The gods had finally decided to punish us for the guilt that ran in our blood.

"I'm growing tired of all this sand and rust, May." Grandma spoke through mouthfuls of sand. She didn't waste her effort trying to spit it out—rust grew in our bones, grit dwelled in our throat. "Too much destruction for the eyes of a wasted old woman like me. There is no better raconteur than I who have told all the stories of the world as it was. If you would, grasp on to them as dearly as if they were your own

memories. Hold on to them even when the future yields no hope."

And so there we hid, in the corner of a wasted building, thousands of years from the time you lived. This is my story, of us standing knee-deep in rust, wading our way through the drifting red dunes, scavenging for what was left so that we may build what the creeping age destroyed. Often, Grandma's blue eyes drifted onwards up to heaven's height, where she was lost in thought of the beautiful past. I would never see with my own eyes the legends of sun-tanned beaches the color of golden-brown sugar, or the glowing green trees that bloom like young girls in May, but you would. Yet the one thing I find perplexing about the people of your time is that you're throwing all this beauty behind your mind as if it's nothing more than worthless fleets of dead rust. Please, I beg you now, watch every rise and fall of the stars, drink all your fresh water, breathe like there's no air to come tomorrow—it's a luxury. Cherish *having* until you don't. Trust me, there is no better raconteur than I.

A Modern Proposal

Eddie Schweikert

Grade 12. Westside High School, Omaha, NE. Liz Hough, Educator. *Silver Key.*

Portfolio Honorable Mention

Congress. The foundation of American representative democracy. A place where over 500 proud, elected Americans meet, divided into two different Houses, various different committees, exponentially more subcommittees, where all real action is lost in a chain of checks and balances. It sometimes seems all our Congressmen and -women do is sit on their bums, twiddling their thumbs, waiting for someone—anyone—to do som'n. Many people agree, our government of today is inefficient. Instead of keeping up with the rapidly more efficient internet and modes of travel, it seems as though it's been working backwards.

So how can this problem be fixed? Obviously our leaders can't be asked, seeing as they'll just put any and all practical ideas through their series of slow subcommittees. So I propose a much better solution: We abolish Congress altogether!

Naturally, in order to accomplish such a feat, a few hurdles have to be jumped. But this is America, and we've done far more difficult things in the past, most notably of all, declaring our independence.

The largest hurdle among them would be amending the Constitution in order to legally throw out the inefficient menace. The Constitution can be amended in one of two ways, both outlined in Article V. One would only expect that none of the 535 Senators or Representatives would propose an amendment that would put them out of work. It is even more unlikely that a ⅔ majority would vote to approve it. But the other way to amend the Constitution is calling a Constitutional Convention of the State Legislatures. Seeing as the States don't like answering to the Federal government anyway, this would likely be much easier than it seems.

The Amendment would, of course, have to become effective immediately, or else Congress would try to find a way to postpone its own demise. They are so well-versed in inefficiency, they would likely face no difficulty in achieving this.

Once written and ratified, there would be no possible opposition, meaning no inefficiency. The Supreme Court cannot rule a Constitutional Amendment unconstitutional because it contradicts the Constitution, because it is in the very nature of an amendment to contradict previously written laws. In addition, the

President plays no role in amending the Constitution, so he would be helpless to stop it, even if he wanted to.

The benefits would be almost instantaneous. Following the initial uproar, it would come to be accepted and viewed as the new normal.

There would be no more failed campaign promises, meaning no one would be disappointed. There would be no Congressmen and -women to make failed promises of their own, and all future Presidents could do anything they wanted without the nasty backlash from Congress.

States would see a much higher level of sovereignty and independence. They would no longer have to answer to the tangled web of Federal mandates, unless the President creates one. If the President does create a regulation the states don't approve of, they have a much higher chance of challenging it, as it is much easier to change the mind of one person than the minds of a body of over 500.

The Supreme Court would also effectively become more efficient, if even still necessary at all. They would no longer have to hear cases that all come down to trivial bickering regarding whether Congress or the President has the authority to do something.

And most importantly of all, elections would become sparser, much less stressful, and much quicker. Voting for one Federal office only every four years is a lot easier and less confusing than voting for some every two, one every four, and a couple more every six. There would be fewer debates between candidates leading up to such elections, as well, because there would be no Congressional candidates to do any debating.

Of course, one might argue voters should simply make better choices when electing members of Congress, to make efficiency and compromise more likely. However, as a nation, we very rarely do this. Inefficiency has become more common because we've allowed it to. For example, we have grown increasingly tolerant of extreme views, hence the increasing polarization of the nation's politics. So why should we be forced to pay more attention, when we can eradicate the scourge altogether?

www.ingramcontent.com/pod-product-compliance
Lightning Source LLC
Chambersburg PA
CBHW070956180726
48291CB00004B/1322

* 9 7 8 1 9 4 2 8 8 5 7 4 0 *

THE DREAMS OF SUMMER DARTSON

PETER PURCHASE

Perth Western Australia

First published in Australia 2024 by Dune Publishing

The Dreams of Summer Dartson

Cataloguing-in-Publication data is available from
The National Library of Australia

General acknowledgement is made to the following for permission to reprint previously published material: Courtesy various artists and other sources held on Alamy, iStock and Shutterstock used for chapter heading photos.

ISBN: 978-0-9756216-6-0 (paperback)
978-0-9756216-7-7 (epub)

Cover photograph: Laurence Mouton – Alamy Stock Photos